Kubernetes

The Ultimate Guide to Learn and Master Kubernetes for Beginners

(Effectively Learn Kubernetes Step-by-step)

Melvin Bennett

Published By **Jordan Levy**

Melvin Bennett

Kubernetes: The Ultimate Guide to Learn and Master Kubernetes for Beginners (Effectively Learn Kubernetes Step-by-step)

ISBN 978-1-7780579-4-6

Legal & Disclaimer

The information contained in this ebook is not designed to replace or take the place of any form of medicine or professional medical advice. The information in this ebook has been provided for educational & entertainment purposes only.

The information contained in this book has been compiled from sources deemed reliable, and it is accurate to the best of the Author's knowledge; however, the Author cannot guarantee its accuracy and validity and cannot be held liable for any errors or omissions. Changes are periodically made to this book. You must consult your doctor or get professional medical advice before using any of the suggested remedies, techniques, or information in this book.

Upon using the information contained in this book, you agree to hold harmless the Author from and against any damages, costs, and expenses, including any legal fees potentially resulting from the application of any of the information provided by this guide. This disclaimer applies to any damages or injury caused by the use and application, whether directly or indirectly, of any advice or information presented, whether for breach of contract, tort, negligence, personal injury, criminal intent, or under any other cause of action.

You agree to accept all risks of using the information presented inside this book. You need to consult a professional medical practitioner in order to ensure you are both able and healthy enough to participate in this program.

Table of contents

Introduction

Emerging cloud computing technologies have evolved more with the open source. New ideas are now becoming technological solutions for enterprises with increasing demands for complex and highly scalable technologies. The advanced cloud ecosystem has become more efficient for both development and IT operations teams of start-ups as well as established enterprises.

Introducing Kubernetes - Technical Overview:

For automated deployment, scaling, monitoring and operations of application cloud containers, it is the most efficient open-source platform. It includes all essential elements with greater scalability options as a complete container-centric infrastructure. Since automation remains the core part of this, professional resource optimizations, adding new features for the end users by scaling up the resources have become more obvious with this option.

Integration through Cloud Containers:

There are many reasons why the enterprises are switching to cloud platforms and containers. To get rid of heavyweight and non-portable architecture; deployment of small, fast yet portable technology platforms are getting the best impact. Instead of hardware virtualizations, the newest way of deploying applications through containers focusing on operating-system-level virtualization. In this way, we can put an end to the limitations of the host through choosing executable file-systems, libraries, and etc.

Adding the most advanced feature of automation of workflow and workload balancing, can be simplified with Kubernetes. Scheduling and running application containers along with developing a container-centric development environment is possible with it. Whether on physical or virtual machines, it can be utilized on all platforms with ease.

Installing and Accessing the Cluster:

Setup or installation of the system varies according to the host OS, through different modules. Kubeadm is used for installations on

Linux, kops for AWS, are the most common options available. Similarly, for accessing the clusters and sharing it through kubeconfig is much easier. Kubeconfig also adds security features to authenticate every access to the clusters.

Its web-based User-Interface or Web UI includes all controls. This dashboard can be accessed remotely for setting up, controlling and monitoring the processes of containers on the clusters. The online user guide and the community that supports this technology are much active to help in installations of the system.
The Ease of Deployment:

With the simplified configuring modules, launching or deploying applications on cloud containers happens on the go. Well management of resources and replication controller has become an essential part of workload deployment and management segment. Performing batch jobs on this cloud environment and the processes of corn jobs can be resourcefully done here.
With Kubernetes, connecting applications with appropriate services through configuring

firewalls of the cloud service providers can be done at once. In complex configurations, creating an external load balancer and use of federated services to discover cross-cluster service. Resource usage monitoring, process logging and like jobs become more accessible with specified modules available on the dashboard. Administrating clusters, installing add-ons, rolling out new features and updates have become more resourceful on a cloud container environment. Configuring or connecting this automated workflow system on other advanced aspects makes the processes more resourceful.

Chapter 1: What Is Kubernetes?

Kubernetes is an open source orchestration tool developed by Google for managing microservices or containerized applications across a distributed cluster of nodes. Kubernetes provides highly resilient infrastructure with zero downtime readying capabilities, automatic rollback, scaling, and self-healing of containers (which consists of auto-placement, auto-restart, auto-replication , and scaling of containers on the basis of hardware usage).

Kubernetes is portable in nature, meaning it can run on numerous public or private cloud platforms such as AWS, Azure, OpenStack, or Apache Mesos. It also runs on bare metal.

Kubernetes Components and Architecture

Kubernetes follows a client-server architecture. It's possible to have a multi-master setup (for high availability), but by default there is a single master server which acts as a controlling node and point of contact. The master server consists of various components including a kube-apiserver, an etcd storage, a kube-controller-manager, a cloud-controller-manager, a kube-scheduler, and a DNS server for Kubernetes services. Node components include kubelet and kube-proxy on top of Docker.

Master Components

Below are the main components found on the master node:

- etcd cluster - a simple, distributed key value storage which is used to store the Kubernetes cluster data (such as number of pods, their state, namespace, etc), API objects and service discovery details. It is only accessible from the API server for security reasons. etcd enables notifications to the cluster about configuration changes with the help of watchers. Notifications are API requests on each etcd cluster node to trigger the update of information in the node's storage.
- kube-apiserver - Kubernetes API server is the central management entity that receives all REST requests for modifications (to pods, services, replication sets/controllers and others), serving as frontend to the cluster. Also, this is the only component that communicates with the etcd cluster, making sure data is stored in etcd and is in agreement with the service details of the deployed pods.
- kube-controller-manager - runs a number of distinct controller processes in the background (for example, replication controller controls

number of replicas in a pod, endpoints controller populates endpoint objects like services and pods, and others) to regulate the shared state of the cluster and perform routine tasks. When a change in a service configuration occurs (for example, replacing the image from which the pods are running, or changing parameters in the configuration yaml file), the controller spots the change and starts working towards the new desired state.

- cloud-controller-manager - is responsible for managing controller processes with dependencies on the underlying cloud provider (if applicable). For example, when a controller needs to check if a node was terminated or set up routes, load balancers or volumes in the cloud infrastructure, all that is handled by the cloud-controller-manager.
- kube-scheduler - helps schedule the pods (a co-located group of containers inside which our application processes are running) on the various nodes based on resource utilization. It reads the service's operational requirements and schedules it on the best fit node. For example, if the application needs 1GB of memory and 2 CPU cores, then the pods for that application will be scheduled on a node with at least those resources. The scheduler runs each time there is a need to schedule pods. The scheduler must know the total resources available as well as resources allocated to existing workloads on each node.

Node (worker) components

Below are the main components found on a (worker) node:

- kubelet - the main service on a node, regularly taking in new or modified pod specifications (primarily through the kube-apiserver) and ensuring that pods and their containers are healthy and running in the desired state. This component also reports to the master on the health of the host where it is running.
- kube-proxy - a proxy service that runs on each worker node to deal with individual host subnetting and expose services to the external world. It performs request forwarding to the correct pods/containers across the various isolated networks in a cluster.

Kubectl
kubectl command is a line tool that interacts with kube-apiserver and send commands to the master node. Each command is converted into an API call.

Kubernetes Concepts

Making use of Kubernetes requires understanding the different abstractions it uses to represent the state of the system, such as services, pods, volumes, namespaces, and deployments.

- Pod - generally refers to one or more containers that should be controlled as a single application. A pod encapsulates application containers, storage resources, a unique network ID and other configuration on how to run the containers.

- Service - pods are volatile, that is Kubernetes does not guarantee a given physical pod will be kept alive (for instance, the replication controller might kill and start a new set of pods). Instead, a service represents a logical set of pods and acts as a gateway, allowing (client) pods to send requests to the service without needing to keep track of which physical pods actually make up the service.
- Volume - similar to a container volume in Docker, but a Kubernetes volume applies to a whole pod and is mounted on all containers in the pod. Kubernetes guarantees data is preserved across container restarts. The volume will be removed only when the pod gets destroyed. Also, a pod can have multiple volumes (possibly of different types) associated.
- Namespace - a virtual cluster (a single physical cluster can run multiple virtual ones) intended for environments with many users spread across multiple teams or projects, for isolation of concerns. Resources inside a namespace must be unique and cannot access resources in a different namespace. Also, a

namespace can be allocated a resource quota to avoid consuming more than its share of the physical cluster's overall resources.

- Deployment - describes the desired state of a pod or a replica set, in a yaml file. The deployment controller then gradually updates the environment (for example, creating or deleting replicas) until the current state matches the desired state specified in the deployment file. For example, if the yaml file defines 2 replicas for a pod but only one is currently running, an extra one will get created. Note that replicas managed via a deployment should not be manipulated directly, only via new deployments.

Kubernetes Design Principles

Kubernetes was designed to support the features required by highly available distributed systems, such as (auto-)scaling, high availability, security and portability.

- Scalability - Kubernetes provides horizontal scaling of pods on the basis of CPU utilization. The threshold for CPU usage is configurable and Kubernetes will automatically start new pods if the threshold is reached. For example, if the threshold is 70% for CPU but the application is actually growing up to 220%, then eventually 3 more pods will be deployed so that the average CPU utilization is back under 70%.

When there are multiple pods for a particular application, Kubernetes provides the load balancing capacity across them. Kubernetes also supports horizontal scaling of stateful pods, including NoSQL and RDBMS databases through Stateful sets. A Stateful set is a similar concept to a Deployment, but ensures storage is persistent and stable, even when a pod is removed.

- High Availability - Kubernetes addresses highly availability both at application and infrastructure level. Replica sets ensure that the desired (minimum) number of replicas of a stateless pod for a given application are running. Stateful sets perform the same role for stateful pods. At the infrastructure level, Kubernetes supports various distributed storage backends like AWS EBS, Azure Disk, Google Persistent Disk, NFS, and more. Adding a reliable, available storage layer to Kubernetes ensures high availability of stateful workloads. Also, each of the master components can be configured for multi-node replication (multi-master) to ensure higher availability.
- Security - Kubernetes addresses security at multiple levels: cluster, application and network. The API endpoints are secured through transport layer security (TLS). Only authenticated users (either service accounts or regular users) can execute operations on the cluster (via API requests). At the application level, Kubernetes secrets can store sensitive information (such as

passwords or tokens) per cluster (a virtual cluster if using namespaces, physical otherwise). Note that secrets are accessible from any pod in the same cluster. Network policies for access to pods can be defined in a deployment. A network policy specifies how pods are allowed to communicate with each other and with other network endpoints.

- Portability - Kubernetes portability manifests in terms of operating system choices (a cluster can run on any mainstream Linux distribution), processor architectures (either virtual machines or bare metal), cloud providers (AWS, Azure or Google Cloud Platform), and new container runtimes, besides Docker, can also be added. Through the concept of federation, it can also support workloads across hybrid (private and public cloud) or multi-cloud environments. This also supports availability zone fault tolerance within a single cloud provider.

WHAT IS KUBERNETES NETWORKING?

Since a Kubernetes cluster consists of various nodes and pods, understanding how they communicate between them is essential. The Kubernetes networking model supports different types of open source implementations. Kubernetes provides an IP address to each pod so that there is no need to map host ports to container ports as in the Docker networking model. Pods behave much like VMs or physical hosts with respect to port allocation, naming, load balancing and application configuration. For more background on Kubernetes components, see Kuberenetes Architecture.

Kubernetes vs. Docker Networking Model

The Docker networking model relies, by default, on a virtual bridge network called Docker0. It is a per-host private network where containers get attached (and thus can reach each other) and allocated a private IP address. This means containers running on different machines are not able to communicate with each other (as they are attached to different hosts' networks). In order to communicate across nodes with Docker, we have to map host ports to container ports and proxy the traffic. In this scenario, it's up to the Docker operator to avoid port clashes between containers.

The Kubernetes networking model, on the other hand, natively supports multi-host networking in which pods are able to communicate with each other by default, regardless of which host they live in. Kubernetes does not provide an implementation of this model by default, rather it relies on third-party tools that comply with the following requirements: all containers are able to communicate with each other without NAT; nodes are able to communicate with containers without NAT; and a container's IP address is the same from inside and outside the container.

Kubernetes follows an "IP-per-pod" model where each pod get assigned an IP address and all containers in a single pod share the same network namespaces and IP address. Containers in the same pod can therefore reach each other's ports via localhost:<port>. However, it is not recommended to communicate directly with a pod via its IP address due to pod's volatility (a pod can be killed and replaced at any moment). Instead, use a Kubernetes service which represents a group of pods acting as a single entity to the outside. Services get allocated their own IP address in the cluster and provide a reliable entry point.

Kubernetes Networking Model Implementations

Kubernetes does not provide a default network implementation, it only enforces a model for third-party tools to implement. There is a variety of implementations nowadays, below we list some popular ones.

- Flannel - a very simple overlay network that satisfies the Kubernetes requirements. Flannel runs an agent on each host and allocates a subnet lease to each of them out of a larger, preconfigured address space.

- Flannel creates a flat network called as overlay network which runs above the host network.
- Project Calico - an open source container networking provider and network policy engine. Calico provides a highly scalable networking and network policy solution for connecting Kubernetes pods based on the same IP networking principles as the internet. Calico can be deployed without encapsulation or overlays to provide high-performance, high-scale data center networking.
- Weave Net - a cloud native networking toolkit which provides a resilient and simple to use (does not require any configuration) network for Kubernetes and its hosted applications. It provides various functionalities like scaling, service discovery, performance without complexity and secure networking.

Other options include Cisco ACI , Cilium , Contiv , Contrail , Kube-router , Nuage , OVN , Romana , VMWare NSX-T with NSX-T Container Plug-in (NCP) . Some tools even support using multiple implementations, such as Huawei CNI-Genie and Multus .

How Pods Communicate with Each Other

Because each pod has a unique IP in a flat address space inside the Kubernetes cluster, direct pod-to-pod communication is possible without requiring any kind of proxy or address translation. This also allows using standard ports for most applications as there is no need to route traffic from a host port to a container port, as in Docker. Note that because all containers in a pod share the same IP address, container-private ports are not possible (containers can access each other's ports via localhost:<port>) and port conflicts are possible. However, the typical use case for a pod is to run a single application service (in a similar fashion to a VM), in which case port conflicts are a rare situation.

How Pods Communicate with Services

Kubernetes services allow grouping pods under a common access policy (for example, load-balanced). The service gets assigned a virtual IP which pods outside the service can communicate with. Those requests are then transparently proxied (via the kube-proxy component that runs on each node) to the pods inside the service. Different proxy-modes are supported:

- iptables : kube-proxy installs iptables rules trap access to service IP addresses and redirect them to the correct pods.

- userspace : kube-proxy opens a port (randomly chosen) on the local node. Requests on this “proxy port” get proxied to one of the service’s pods (as retrieved from Endpoints API).

- ipvs (from Kubernetes 1.9): calls netlink interface to create ipvs rules and regularly synchronizes them with the Endpoints API.

Kubernetes also offers an Endpoints API for Kubernetes native applications that is updated whenever the set of pods in a service changes. This allows a pod to retrieve the current endpoints for all pods in a service.

Incoming Traffic from the Outside World

Nodes inside a Kubernetes cluster are firewalled from the Internet by default, thus services IP addresses are only targetable within the cluster network. In order to allow incoming traffic from outside the cluster, a service specification can map the service to one or more externalIPs (external to the cluster). Requests arriving at an external IP address get routed by the underlying cloud provider to a node in the cluster (usually via a load balancer outside Kubernetes). The node then knows which service is mapped to the external IP and also which pods are part of the service, thus routing the request to an appropriate pod.

To support more complex policies on incoming traffic, Kubernetes provides an Ingress API offering externally-reachable URLs, traffic load balancing, SSL termination, and name based virtual hosting to services. An ingress is a collection of rules that allow inbound connections to reach the cluster service. Note that to actually action ingresses specified via the API, an ingress controller (such as the NGINX ingress controller) must be deployed and configured for the cluster. This might be done automatically or not, depending on which Kubernetes cloud provider you are using.

DNS for Services and Pods

Kubernetes provides its own DNS service to resolve domain names inside the cluster in order for pods to communicate with each other. This is implemented by deploying a regular Kubernetes service which does name resolution inside the cluster, and configuring individual containers to contact the DNS service to resolve domain names. Note that this “internal DNS” is compatible and expected to run along with the cloud provider’s DNS service.

Every service gets assigned a DNS name which resolves to the cluster IP of the service. The naming convention includes the service name and its namespace. For example:

my-service.my-namespace.svc.cluster.local

A pod inside the same namespace as the service does not need to fully qualify its name, for example a pod in my-namespace could lookup this service with a DNS query for my-service , while a pod outside my-namespace would have to query for my-service.my-namespace .

For headless services (without a cluster IP), the DNS name resolves to the set of IPs of the pods which are part of the service. The caller can then use the set of IPs as it sees fit (for example round-robin).

By default pods get assigned a DNS name which includes the pod's IP address and namespace. In order to assign a more meaningful DNS name, the pod's specification can specify a hostname and subdomain:

Network Extensions

Network extensions are the way to extend or enhance the networking by introducing various network functionalities such as cross-node networking or network policies. There are two types of network extensions or plugins:

- CNI plugin: designed for interoperability, this plugin implements the Container Network

Interface (CNI) specification inserting a network interface into the container network namespace (e.g. one end of a veth pair) and making any necessary changes on the host (for example, attaching the other end of the veth into a bridge).

- Kubenet plugin : a simple plugin for Linux usage only, typically used together with a cloud provider that sets up routing rules for communication between nodes.

INTRODUCTION TO KUBERNETES MONITORING

Introduction

With over 40,000 stars on Github, more than 70,000 commits, and with major contributors like Google and Redhat, Kubernetes has rapidly taken over the container ecosystem to become the true leader of container orchestration platforms.

Understanding Kubernetes and Its Abstractions

At the infrastructure level, a Kubernetes cluster is a set of physical or virtual machines acting in a specific role. The machines acting in the role of Master act as the brain of all operations and are charged with orchestrating containers that run on all of the Nodes.

Master components manage the lifecycle of a pod, the base unit of deployment within a

Kubernetes cluster. If a pod dies, the Controller creates a new one. If you scale the number of pod replicas up or down, the Controller creates or destroys pods to satisfy your request. The Master role includes the following components:

- kube-apiserver - exposes APIs for the other master components.
- etcd - a consistent and highly-available key/value store used for storing all internal cluster data.
- kube-scheduler - uses information in the Pod spec to decide on which Node to run a Pod.
- kube-controller-manager - responsible for Node management (detecting if a Node fails), pod replication, and endpoint creation.
- cloud-controller-manager - runs controllers that interact with the underlying cloud providers.

Node components are worker machines in Kubernetes and are managed by the Master. A node may be a virtual machine (VM) or physical machine, and Kubernetes runs equally well on both types of systems. Each node contains the necessary components to run pods:

- kubelet: handles all communication between the Master and the node on which it is running. It interfaces with the container runtime to deploy and monitor containers.

- kube-proxy: maintains the network rules on the host and handles transmission of packets between pods, the host, and the outside world.
- container runtime: responsible for running containers on the host. The most popular engine is Docker, although Kubernetes supports container runtimes from rkt, runc and others.

From a logical perspective, a Kubernetes deployment is comprised of various components, each serving a specific purpose within the cluster.

- Pods are the basic unit of deployment within Kubernetes. A pod consists of one or more containers that share the same network namespace and IP address. Best practices recommend that you create one pod per application component so you can scale and control them separately.
- Services provide a consistent IP address in front of a set of pods and a policy that controls access to them. The set of pods targeted by a service is often determined by a label selector. This makes it easy to point the service to a different set of pods during upgrades or blue/green deployments.

- ReplicaSets are controlled by deployments and ensure that the desired number of pods for that deployment are running.

- Namespaces define a logical namespace for resources such as pods and services. They enable resources to use the same names, whereas resources in a single namespace must have unique names. Rancher uses namespaces with its role-based access control to provide a secure separation between namespaces and the resources running inside of them.

- Metadata marks containers based on their deployment characteristics.

Monitoring Kubernetes

Multiple services and namespaces can be spread across the infrastructure. As seen above, each of the services are made of pods, which can have one or more containers inside. With so many moving parts, monitoring even a small Kubernetes cluster can present a challenge. It requires a deep understanding of the application architecture and functionality in order to monitor it effectively.

Kubernetes ships with tools for monitoring the cluster:

Probes actively monitor the health of a container. If the probe determines that a container is no longer healthy, the probe will restart it.

cAdvisor is an open source agent that monitors resource usage and analyzes the performance of containers. Originally created by Google, cAdvisor is now integrated with the Kubelet. It collects, aggregates, processes and exports metrics such as CPU, memory, file and network usage for all containers running on a given node.

The kubernetes dashboard is an add-on which gives an overview of the resources running on your cluster. It also gives a very basic means of deploying and interacting with those resources. Kubernetes has tremendous capability for automatically recovering from failures. It can restart pods if a process crashes, and it will redistribute pods if a node fails. However, for all of its power, there are times when it cannot fix a problem. In order to detect those situations, we need additional monitoring.

Layers Of Monitoring

Infrastructure

All clusters should have monitoring of the underlying server components because problems at the server level will show up in the workloads.

What to monitor?

- CPU utilization. Monitoring the CPU will reveal both system and user consumption, and it will also show iowait. When running clusters in the cloud or with any network storage, iowait will indicate bottlenecks waiting for storage reads and writes (i/o processes). An oversubscribed storage framework can impact performance.

- Memory usage. Monitoring memory will show how much memory is in use and how much is available, either as free memory or as cache. Systems that run up against memory limits will begin to swap (if swap is available on the system), and swapping will rapidly degrade performance.

- Disk pressure. If a system is running write-intensive services like etcd or any datastore, running out of disk space can be catastrophic. The inability to write data will result in corruption, and that corruption can transfer to real-world losses. Technologies like LVM make it trivial to grow disk space as needed, but keeping an eye on it is imperative.

- Network bandwidth. In today's era of gigabit interfaces, it might seem like you can never run out of bandwidth. However, it doesn't take more than a few aberrant services, a data breach, system compromise, or DOS attack to eat up all of the bandwidth and cause an outage. Keeping awareness of your normal data consumption and the patterns of your application will help you keep costs down and also aid in capacity planning.

- Pod resources. The Kubernetes scheduler works best when it knows what resources a pod needs. It can then assure that it places pods on nodes where the resources are available. When designing your network, consider how many nodes can fail before the remaining nodes can no longer run all of the desired resources. Using a service such as a cloud autoscaling group will make recovery quick, but be sure that the remaining nodes can handle the increased load for the time that it takes to bring the failed node back online.

Kubernetes Services

All of the components that make up a Kubernetes Master or Worker, including etcd, are critical to the health of your applications. If any of these fail, the monitoring system needs to detect the failure and either fix it or send an alert.

Internal Services

The final layer is that of the Kubernetes resources themselves. Kubernetes exposes metrics about the resources, and we can also monitor the applications directly. Although we can trust that Kubernetes will work to maintain the desired state, if it's unable to do so, we need a way for a human to intervene and fix the issue.

Monitoring with Rancher

In addition to managing Kubernetes clusters running anywhere, on any provider, Rancher will also monitor the resources running inside of those clusters and send alerts when they exceed defined thresholds.

There are already dozens of tutorials on how to deploy Rancher. If you don't already have a cluster running, pause here and visit our quickstart guide to spin one up. When it's running, return here to continue with monitoring.

The cluster overview gives you an idea of the resources in use and the state of the Kubernetes components. In our case, we're using 78% of the CPU, 26% of the RAM and 11% of the maximum number of pods we can run within the cluster.

When you select the name of the workload, Rancher presents a page that shows information about it. At the top of this page it will show you each of the pods, which node they're on, their IP address, and their state. Clicking on any individual pod takes us one level deeper, where now we see detailed information about only that pod. The hamburger menu icon in the top right corner lets us interact with the pod, and through this we can execute a shell, view the logs, or delete the pod.

Use Prometheus for Monitoring

The information visible in the Rancher UI is useful for troubleshooting, but it's not the best way to actively track the state of the cluster throughout every moment of its life. For that we'll use Prometheus, a sibling project of Kubernetes under the care and guidance of the Cloud Native Computing Foundation. We'll also use Grafana, a tool for converting time-series data into beautiful graphs and dashboards.

Prometheus is an open-source application for monitoring systems and generating alerts. It can monitor almost anything, from servers to applications, databases, or even a single process. In the Prometheus lexicon it monitors targets, and each unit of a target is called a metric. The act of retrieving information about a target is known as scraping. Prometheus will scrape targets at designated intervals and store the information in a time-series database. Prometheus has its own scripting language called PromQL.

Grafana is also open source and runs as a web application. Although frequently used with Prometheus, it also supports backend datastores such as InfluxDB, Graphite, Elasticsearch, and others. Grafana makes it easy to create graphs and assemble those graphs into dashboards. Those dashboards can be protected by a strong authentication and authorization layer, and they can also be shared with others without giving them access to the server itself. Grafana makes heavy use of JSON for its object definitions, which makes its graphs and dashboards extremely portable and easy to use with version control.

KUBERNETES MONITORING

Understanding Kubernetes monitoring pipeline(s) is essential to help you diagnose run-time problems and to manage the scale of your pods, and cluster. Monitoring is one of these areas that are evolving very rapidly inside Kubernetes. It has a lot of pieces that are still in the influx and hence some confusion. My goal as I hope in this chapter is to clarify it a bit and to give you a good starting point.

Kubernetes has two monitoring pipelines: (1) The core metrics pipeline, which is an integral part of Kubernetes and always installed with all distributions, and (2) The services monitoring (non-core) pipeline, which is a separate pipeline, and Kubernetes has no or limited dependency on. Keep reading to learn why :)

Core Monitoring Pipeline

Sometimes is referred to as the resource metrics pipeline. The core monitoring pipeline is installed with every distribution. It provides enough details to other components inside the Kubernetes cluster to run as expected, such as the scheduler to allocate pods and containers, HPA and VPA to take proper decisions scaling pods.

The way it works is relatively simple:

- CAdvisor collects metrics about containers and nodes that on which it is installed. Note: CAdvisor is installed by default on all cluster nodes
- Kubelet exposes these metrics (default is one-minute resolution) through Kubelet APIs.
- Metrics Server discovers all available nodes and calls Kubelet API to get containers and nodes resources usage.
- Metrics Server exposes these metrics through Kubernetes aggregation API.

A few helpful points

- Kubelet cannot run without CAdvisor. If you try to uninstall it or stop it, the cluster's behavior will become unpredictable.
- Even though Heapster "soon to be deprecated" is currently dependent on CAdvisor, but CAdvisor is not going away anytime soon.

Services Monitoring Pipeline

Services pipeline in abstract terms is relatively simple. Confusion usually comes from the plethora of services, agents that you can mix and match to get your pipeline up and running. Also, you can blame Heapster for that :)

Services Monitoring Pipeline consists of three main components: (1) Collection agent, (2) Metrics Server, and (3) Dashboards. I'll not talk about alerting because it has lots of interesting twists :)

Below is the typical workflow, including most common components

- Monitoring agent collects node metrics. cAdvisor collects containers and pods metrics.
- Monitoring Aggregation service collects data from its own agent and cAdvisor.
- Data is stored in the monitoring system's storage.

- Monitoring aggregation service exposes metrics through APIs and dashboards.

A Few Notes:

- Prometheus is the official monitoring server sponsored and incubated by CNCF. It integrates directly with cAdvisor. You don't need to install a 3rd party agent to retrieve additional metrics about your containers. However, if you need deeper insights about each node, you need to install an agent of your choice — see Prometheus integrations and third-party exporters page.
- Almost all monitoring systems piggyback on Kubernetes scheduling and orchestration. For example, their agents are installed as DeomonSets and depend on Kubernetes scheduler to have an instance scheduled on each node.
- Most monitoring agents depend on Kubelet to collect container relevant metrics, which in turn depends on cAdvisor. Very few agents collect container relevant details independently.
- Most monitoring aggregation services depend on agents pushing metrics to them. Prometheus is an exception. It pulls metrics out of the installed agents.

What should you consider in Kubernetes Services Pipeline?

Ideal Services pipeline depends on two main factors: (1) collection of relevant metrics, (2) Awareness of continuous changes inside kubernetes cluster.
A good pipeline should focus on collecting relevant metrics. There are plenty of agents that can collect OS and process-level metrics. But you will find very few out there that can collect details about containers running at a given node, such as the number of running containers, container state, docker engine metrics, etc. cAdvisor is the best agent IMO for this job so far.
Awareness of continuous changes means that the monitoring pipeline is aware of different pods, containers instances and can relate them to their parent entities, i.e. Deployment, Statefulsets, Namespace, etc. It also means that the metrics server is aware of system-wide metrics that should be visible to users, such as the number of pending pods, nodes status, etc.
What about Metrics Visualization?

You can visualize metrics in many different ways. The most common open source tool that easily integrates with Prometheus is Grafana. The challenges you will face though is building proper dashboards to monitor the right metrics. That said, you should have dashboards monitoring the following:

- Cluster level capacity utilization, this shows how much CPU memory being across the whole cluster and per node.
- Kubernetes Orchestration Metrics, which tracks the status of your pods and containers inside your cluster. This includes the distribution of pods among nodes.
- Kubernetes Core Services, which visualizes the status of critical services such as CoreDNS, Calico, and any other service important for networking, storage, and pods scheduling.
- Application Specific Metrics, which tracks the status of your apps. They should reflect your users' experience and business critical metrics.

Note: You can get started with this Grafana template dashboards for Kubernetes.

- Grafana is not best suited for alerting. I see a lot of teams depend on it to create alerting rules. However, it is not as reliable and comprehensive as Prometheus alerting manager.

Changes To Watch For

Heapster is Going Away

Heapster is currently causing some confusion given that it is used to show both core pipeline metrics and services metrics. In reality, you can remove Heapster and nothing bad will happen to the core Kubernetes scheduling and orchestration scenarios. It was the default monitoring pipeline and I guess it still is the default in a lot of distributions. But you don't have to use it at all.

So, the Kubernetes community wanted to make the separation clearer between core and services monitoring pipelines. Hence, Heapster will be deprecated and replaced by the Metrics Server (MS) as the main source of aggregated core metrics. Think of the MS as a trimmed down version of Heapster. Major immediate changes are: (1) No historical data or queries, (2) eliminating a lot of container-specific metrics, pod focus metrics only. Metrics Server is meant to provide core metrics that are needed for core Kubernetes scenarios, such as autoscaling, scheduling, etc., likely to take place in 2019 releases.

Metrics Server Will Get More Cool Features

Infrastore will store Metric Server historical data with a support of simple SQL-like queries. It will support initially metrics collected by the Metrics Server. My guess, because Kubernetes community love extensibility, they will make it extensible and allow custom metrics to be added to the Metrics Server and its store.

TL;DR

- You need to differentiate between core metrics pipeline and the services pipeline.
- Heapster will be deprecated. you should pick the best pipeline that works for your needs.
- The community official tool is Prometheus. You can use a variety of other open source or commercial tools, but I recommend to get started with Prometheus before you decide with any other tools that may cost you a lot down the road.
- Use Grafana for metrics visualization. But I wouldn't recommend using it for alerting.

Chapter 2: Top Open-Source Tools For Monitoring Kubernetes

Distributed computing and orchestration have solved many problems, but they also have created new challenges. While a Kubernetes cluster appears to a user to be a single computer, it is actually a set of independent nodes and multiple services that have been connected.

With this new way of building and running applications, your monitoring and observability strategies need to change—and so will the tools you use. Here are the most popular and most reliable open-source monitoring tools you can choose from when working with Kubernetes.

1. Kubelet

In a Kubernetes cluster, Kubelet acts as a bridge between the master and the nodes. It is the primary node agent that runs on each node and maintains a set of pods. Kubelet watches for PodSpecs via the Kubernetes API server and collects resource utilization statistics and pod and events status.

Kubelet fetches individual container usage statistics from Docker's Container Advisor (cAdvisor). But Kubelet also accepts PodSpecs provided through different mechanisms and ensures that the containers described in those PodSpecs are up and running. These aggregated pod resource usage statistics are exposed via a REST API.

2. Container Advisor (cAdvisor)

cAdvisor is a container resource usage and performance analysis agent; it's integrated into the Kubelet binary. cAdvistor auto-discovers all containers in a machine and collects statistics about memory, network usage, filesystem, and CPU. cAdvisor has native support for Docker containers. It does not operate at the pod level, but on each node.

Be advised, however: cAdvisor is a simple-to-use but limited tool, so if you are looking to store metrics for long-term use or perform complex monitoring actions, cAdvisor will not fit your needs.

3. Kube-state-metrics

Kube-state-metrics listens to the Kubernetes API server and generates metrics about the state of numerous Kubernetes objects, including cron jobs, config maps, pods, and nodes. These metrics are unmodified, unlike kubectl metrics that use the same Kubernetes API but apply some heuristics to display comprehensible and readable messages.

Kube-state-metrics uses the Golang Prometheus client to export metrics in the Prometheus metrics exposition format and expose metrics on an HTTP endpoint. Prometheus can consume the web endpoint.
This tool is not oriented toward performance and health but rather toward cluster-wide, state-based metrics such as the number of desired pod replicas for deployment or the total CPU resources available on a node.

4. Kubernetes Dashboard

Kubernetes Dashboard is a web-based, UI add-on for Kubernetes clusters. It has many features that allow users to create and manage workloads as well as do discovery, load balancing, configuration, storage, and monitoring. It is helpful for small clusters and for people starting to learn Kubernetes.

This tool offers different views for CPU and memory usage metrics aggregated across all nodes. It can also be used to monitor the health status of workloads (pods, deployments, replica sets, cron jobs, etc.). Installing Kubernetes Dashboard is quite easy and can be done using ready-to-use YAML files.

5. Prometheus

Prometheus is one of the most popular monitoring tools used with Kubernetes. It's community-driven and a member of the Cloud Native Computing Foundation. This project, developed first by SoundCloud and afterward donated to the CNCF, is inspired by Google Borg Monitor.

Prometheus stores all its data as a time series. This data can be queried via the PromQL query language and visualized with a built-in expression browser. Since Prometheus is not a dashboard, it relies on Grafana for visualizing data.

Version 1.0 of this tool was released in 2016, and it is becoming one of the most used Kubernetes monitoring tools. Other tools from the Kubernetes ecosystem, including Istio, include a built-in Prometheus adapter that exposes generated metrics.
Prometheus can be installed directly as a single binary that you can run on your host or as a Docker container. Running Prometheus on top of Kubernetes can be easily accomplished with the Prometheus Operator.

6. Jaeger

Jaeger is a tracing system released by Uber Technologies; it's used for troubleshooting and monitoring transactions in complex distributed systems.

With the rise of microservices and distributed systems, problems can include distributed context propagation, distributed transactions monitoring, and latency optimization. Jaeger addresses these problems as well as others that we can find in distributed systems.

Jaeger has native support for OpenTracing and addresses two main areas: networking and observability.

7. Kubewatch

Kubewatch is a Kubernetes watcher that publishes event notifications in a Slack channel. This tool allows you to specify the resources you want to monitor. It is written in Golang and uses a Kubernetes client library to interact with a Kubernetes API server.

Using a simple YAML file, you can choose the resources to watch, including daemon sets, deployments, pods, replica sets, replication controllers, services, secrets, and configuration maps.

8. Weave Scope

Weave Scope is a zero-configuration monitoring tool developed by Weaveworks. It generates a map of processes, containers, and hosts in a Kubernetes cluster to help understand Docker containers in real time. It can also be used to manage containers and run diagnostic commands on containers without leaving the graphical UI.

If you are looking for a practical graphical tool to obtain a visual overview of your Kubernetes cluster—including the application, the infrastructure, and the connections among your cluster nodes—Weave Scope may help you.

This tool is extensible via some plugins.

9. The EFK Stack

The EFK stack comprises Fluentd, Elasticsearch, and Kibana.

These tools work well with one another and together represent a reliable solution used for Kubernetes monitoring and log aggregation.

Fluentd collects logs from pods running on cluster nodes, then routes them to a centralized Elasticsearch. Then Elasticsearch ingests these logs from Fluentd and stores them in a central location. It is also used to efficiently search text files.

Kibana is the UI; the user can visualize the collected logs and metrics and create custom dashboards based on queries.

The EFK stack is useful for troubleshooting logs, dashboarding, and detecting issues as they come up—all in a user-friendly interface.

KUBERNETES MONITORING: BEST PRACTICES, METHODS, AND EXISTING SOLUTIONS

Monitoring an application's current state is one of the most effective ways to anticipate problems and discover bottlenecks in a production environment. Yet it is also currently one of the biggest challenges faced by almost all software development organizations. Deadlines, inexperience, culture, and management are just some of the obstacles that can affect how successful teams are at overcoming this challenge.

The growing adoption of microservices makes logging and monitoring more complex since a large number of applications, distributed and diversified in nature, are communicating with each other. A single point of failure can stop the entire process, but identifying it is becoming increasingly difficult.

Monitoring, of course, is just one challenge Microservices pose. Handling availability, performance, and deployments are pushing teams to create, or use, orchestrators to handle all the services and servers. There are several cluster orchestration tools, but Kubernetes (K8S) is becoming increasingly popular when compared to its competitors. A container orchestration tool such as Kubernetes handles containers in several computers, and removes the complexity of handling distributed processing.

But how does one monitor such a tool? There are so many variables to keep track of that we need new tools, new techniques, and new methods to effectively capture the data that matters.

Why Monitor Kubernetes and What Metrics Can Be Measured

As mentioned, Kubernetes is the most popular container orchestrator currently available. It is officially available in major clouds provided by Google, Azure, and, more recently AWS, and it can run in a local, bare metal data center. Even Docker has embraced Kubernetes and is now offering it as part of some of their packages.

Generally speaking, there are several Kubernetes metrics to monitor. These can be separated into two main components: (1) monitoring the cluster itself, and (2) monitoring pods.

Cluster Monitoring

For cluster monitoring, the objective is to monitor the health of the entire Kubernetes cluster. As an administrator, we are interested in discovering if all the nodes in the cluster are working properly and at what capacity, how many applications are running on each node, and the resource utilization of the entire cluster.

Allow me to highlight some of the measurable metrics:

- Node resource utilization – there are many metrics in this area, all related to resource utilization. Network bandwidth, disk utilization, CPU, and memory utilization are examples of this. Using these metrics, one can find out whether or not to increase or decrease the number and size of nodes in the cluster.
- The number of nodes – the number of nodes available is an important metric to follow. This allows you to figure out what you are paying for (if you are using cloud providers), and to discover what the cluster is being used for.
- Running pods – the number of pods running will show you if the number of nodes

available is sufficient and if they will be able to handle the entire workload in case a node fails.

Pod Monitoring

The act of monitoring a pod can be separated into three categories: (1) Kubernetes metrics, (2) container metrics, and (3) application metrics.

Using Kubernetes metrics, we can monitor how a specific pod and its deployment are being handled by the orchestrator. The following information can be monitored: the number of instances a pod has at the moment and how many were expected (if the number is low, your cluster may be out of resources), how the on-progress deployment is going (how many instances were changed from an older version to a new one), health checks, and some network data available through network services.

Container metrics are available mostly through Cadvisor and exposed by Heapster, which queries every node about the running containers. In this case, metrics like CPU, network, and memory usage compared with the maximum allowed are the highlights.

Finally, there are the application specific metrics. These metrics are developed by the application itself and are related to the business rules it addresses. For example, a database application will probably expose metrics related to an indices' state and statistics concerning tables and relationships. An e-commerce application would expose data concerning the number of users online and how much money the software made in the last hour, for example.

The metrics described in the latter type are commonly exposed directly by the application: if you want to keep closer track you should connect the application to a monitoring application.

Monitoring Kubernetes Methods

I'd like to mention two main approaches to collecting metrics from your cluster and exporting them to an external endpoint. As a guiding rule, the metric collection should be handled consistently over the entire cluster. Even if the system has nodes deployed in several places all over the world or in a hybrid cloud, the system should handle the metrics collection in the same way, with the same reliability.

Method 1 – Using DaemonSets

One approach to monitoring all cluster nodes is to create a special kind of Kubernetes pod called DaemonSets. Kubernetes ensures that every node created has a copy of the DaemonSet pod, which virtually enables one deployment to watch each machine in the cluster. As nodes are destroyed, the pod is also terminated. Many monitoring solutions use the DaemonSet structure to deploy an agent on every cluster node. In this case, there is not a general solution — each tool will have its own software for cluster monitoring.

Method 2 – Using Heapster

Heapster, on the other hand, is a uniform platform adopted by Kubernetes to generally send monitoring metrics to a system. Heapster is a bridge between a cluster and a storage designed to collect metrics. The supported storages are listed here.

Unlike DaemonSets, Heapster acts as a normal pod and discovers every cluster node via the Kubernetes API. Using Kubelet (a tool that enables master-node communications) and cAdvisor (a container monitoring tool that collects metrics for each running container), the bridge can store all relevant information about the cluster and its containers.
A cluster can consist of thousands of nodes, and an even greater amount of pods. It is virtually impossible to observe each one on a normal basis so it is important to create multiple labels for each deployment. For example, creating a label for database intensive pods will enable the

operator to identify if there is a problem with the database service.

Comparing Monitoring Solutions

Let's take a look at five common monitoring solutions used by Kubernetes users. The first two tools (Heapster/InfluxDB/Grafana and Prometheus/Grafana) combine open source tools that are deployed inside Kubernetes. For the third option (Heapster/ELK) you can use your own ELK Stack or a hosted solution like Logz.io's. The last two options reviewed here (Datadog/Dynatrace) are proprietary APM solutions that provide Kubernetes monitoring.

The examples below are provided here. They use an Azure Container Service instance, but should work in any Kubernetes deployment without too many changes. As part of the testing process, a pod is deployed with a function randomly logging messages.

Heapster, InfluxDB, and Grafana

The most straightforward solution to monitor your Kubernetes cluster is by using a combination of Heapster to collect metrics, InfluxDB to store it in a time series database, and Grafana to present and aggregate the collected information.

The Heapster GIT project has the files needed to deploy this design.

Basically, as part of this solution, you'll deploy InfluxDB and Grafana, and edit the Heapster deployment to send data to InfluxDB. Use the command

Grafana is an extremely flexible tool and you can combine several metrics into a useful dashboard for yourself. In the example above, we captured the metrics provided by Kubernetes and Docker (via cAdvisor). They are generic metrics that every node and every pod will have, but you can also add specific metrics for applications.
Prometheus and Grafana

Prometheus is another popular solution for collecting Kubernetes metrics, with several tools, frameworks, and API's available for using it.

Since Prometheus does not have a Heapster sink, you can use InfluxDB and Prometheus together for the same Grafana instance, collecting different metrics, whenever each one is easier to collect.
Heapster + ELK Stack

The ELK Stack is a combination of three components: Elasticsearch, Logstash, and Kibana, each responsible for a different stage in the data pipeline. ELK is a widely used for centralized logging, but can also be used for collecting and monitoring metrics.

There are various methods of hooking in ELK with our Kubernetes. One method, for example, uses deploys fluentd as a DaemonSet. In the example below, however, we will simply create an Elasticsearch sink for Heapster.

Needless to say, the example above is an overly simple Elasticsearch instance that is not designed for scalability and high availability. And if you are monitoring a cluster, you should also consider not storing the data inside the same cluster as this will affect computed metrics, and you will not be able to investigate issues in case the cluster is down. A cloud-based ELK solution such as Logz.io can be used as a secure and reliable ELK endpoint that will automatically scale as your data grows.

Metricbeat is another ELK monitoring solution that is worth mentioning and will be reviewed in a future post. This solution involves installing Metricbeat on each monitored server to send metrics to Elasticsearch. A Kubernetes module for Metricbeat is still in the beta phase, but you can already use this shipper to monitor your cluster, nodes, and pods.

Datadog

Proprietary APM solutions like Datadog aim to simplify monitoring by enabling organizations to monitor their applications and infrastructure more easily. By definition, these systems are designed so that setting up a data pipeline is as effortless as possible, a simplicity that will often come at a cost.

To start using Datadog for monitoring your Kubernetes cluster, simply create an account, and access the Integrations → Agents area. Search for Kubernetes, and select the displayed result.

Dynatrace

Dynatrace is another APM solution that provides an agent that will run as a DaemonSet in your cluster. The steps to have a Dynatrace agent deployed are less straightforward since you have to collect data from more than one page until you have a proper deployment file.

Once you have the file deployed using

you'll have metrics flowing to Dynatrace in a few minutes.

Dynatrace does not distinguish between a simple Linux host and Kubernetes nodes, so you can't expect some useful Kubernetes metrics exposed by default like with Datadog.

THE STATE OF KUBERNETES CONFIGURATION MANAGEMENT: AN UNSOLVED PROBLEM

Configuration management is a hard, unsolved problem. When we first started Argo CD, a GitOps deployment tool for Kubernetes, we knew we had to limit its scope to a deployment tool and not go anywhere near config management. We understood that since there was no perfect config management solution, Argo CD should remain agnostic to how kubernetes manifests are rendered, and let the user decide for themselves the right tool and workflow that works best for them.

Good Kubernetes configuration tools have the following properties:

- Declarative. The config is unambiguous, deterministic and not system dependent.
- Readable. The config is written in a way that is easy to understand.
- Flexible. The tool helps facilitates, and does not get in the way of accomplishing what you are trying to do.
- Maintainable. The tool should promote reuse and composability.

A couple of key reasons Kubernetes config management is so challenging: what sounds like a simple act of deploying an application, can have wildly different, even opposing requirements, and it's difficult for a single tool to accommodate all such requirements. Imagine the following use cases:

A cluster operator who deploys 3rd-party, off-the-shelf applications, such as Wordpress, to their cluster with little to no customization of those apps. The most important criteria for this user is to easily receive updates from an upstream source and upgrade their application as easily and seamlessly as possible (e.g. new versions, security patches, etc...).

A SaaS application developer who deploys their bespoke application to one or more environments (e.g. dev, staging, prod-west, prod-east). These environments may be spread across different accounts, clusters, and namespaces with subtle differences between them, so configuration re-use is paramount. For these users, it is important to go from a Git commit in their code base to deploying to each of their environments in a fully automated way, and manage the configuration of their environments in a straightforward and maintainable way. These developers have zero interest in semantic versioning of their releases since they might be deploying multiple times a day, and the notion of a major, minor and patch versions ultimately have no meaning for their application.

As you can see, these are completely different use cases, and more often than not, a tool which excels at one, doesn't handle the other very well. After having built first class support in Argo CD for a few of the more popular config tools (Helm, kustomize, ksonnet, jsonnet), and having used these tools at Intuit to manage various applications in our clusters, we've accumulated some unique insights about the strengths and weaknesses of each.

Helm

Let's start with the obvious one, Helm, which needs no introduction. Love it or hate it, Helm, being the first one on the scene, is an integral part of the Kubernetes ecosystem, and chances are that at one point or another you've installed something by runninghelm install.

The important thing note about Helm is that it is a self-described package manager for Kubernetes, and doesn't claim to be a configuration management tool. However, since many people use Helm templating for exactly this purpose, it belongs in the discussion. These users invariably end up maintaining several values.yaml, one for each environment (e.g. values-base.yaml, values-prod.yaml, values-dev.yaml), then parameterize their chart in such a way that environment specific values can be used in the chart. This method more or less works, but it makes the templates unwieldy, since golang templating is flat, and needs to support every conceivable parameter for each environment, which ultimately litters the entire template with {{-if / else}} switches.

The Good:

There's a chart for that. Undoubtedly, Helm's biggest strength is its excellent chart repository. Just recently, we had the need to run a highly available Redis, without a persistent volume, to be used as a throwaway cache. There's something to be said about just being able to throw the redis-ha chart into your namespace, set persistentVolume.enabled: false, point your service at it, and someone else has already done the hard work of figuring out how to run Redis reliably on a Kubernetes cluster.

The Bad:

Golang templating. "Look that that beautiful and elegant helm template!", said no one ever. It is well known that Helm templates suffer from a readability problem. I don't doubt that this will be addressed with Helm 3's support for Lua, but until then, well, I hope you like curly braces.

Complicated SaaS CD pipelines. For SaaS CI/CD pipelines, assuming you are using Helm the way it is intended (i.e. using Tiller), an automated deploy in your pipeline might go several ways.

But in the worst case, where existing chart parameters cannot support your desired manifest changes, you go through a whole song and dance of bundling a new a Helm chart, bumping its semvers, publishing it to a chart repository, and redeploying with a helm upgrade. In the Linux world, this is analogous to building a new RPM, publishing the RPM to a yum repository, then running yum install, all so you can get your shiny new CLI into /usr/bin. While this model works great for packaging and distribution, in the case of bespoke SaaS applications, it's an unnecessarily complex and a roundabout way to deploy your applications. For this reason, many people choose to run helm template and pipe the output to kubectl apply, but at that point you are better off using some other tool that is specifically designed for this purpose.

Non-declarative by default. If you ever added --set param=value to any one of your Helm deploys, I'm sorry to tell you that your deployment process is not declarative. These values are only recorded in the Helm ConfigMap netherworld (and maybe your bash history), so hopefully you wrote those down somewhere. This is far from ideal if you ever need to recreate your cluster from scratch. A slightly better way would be to record all parameters in a new custom values.yaml which you can store in Git and deploy using -f my-values.yaml. However, this is annoying when you're deploying an OTS chart from Helm stable, and you don't have an obvious place to store that values.yaml side-by-side to the relevant chart. The best solution that I've come up with, is to compose a new dummy chart which has the upstream chart as a dependency. Still, I have yet to find a canonical way of updating a parameter in a values.yaml in a pipeline using a one-liner, short of running sed.

Kustomize

Kustomize was created around the design principles described in Brian Grant's excellent dissertation regarding Declarative Application Management. Kustomize has seen a meteoric rise in popularity, and in the eight months since it started, has already been merged into kubectl. Whether or not you agree with the manner in which it was merged, it goes without saying that kustomize applications will now have a permanent mainstay in the Kubernetes ecosystem and will be the default choice that

users will gravitate towards for config management. Yes, it helps to be part of kubectl!
The Good:

No parameters & templates. Kustomize apps are extremely easy to reason about, and I dare say, a pleasure to look at. It's about as close as you can get to Kubernetes YAML since the overlays that you compose to perform customizations are basically subsets of Kubernetes YAML.

The Bad:

No parameters & templates. The same property that makes kustomize applications so readable, can also make it very limiting. For example, I was recently trying to get the kustomize CLI to set an image tag for a custom resource instead of a Deployment, but was unable to. Kustomize does have a concept of "vars," which look a lot like parameters, but somehow aren't, and can only be used in Kustomize's sanctioned whitelist of field paths. I feel like this is one of those times when the solution, despite making the hard things easy, ends up making the easy things hard.

Jsonnet

Jsonnet is actually a language and not really a "tool." Furthermore, its use is not specific to Kubernetes (although it's been popularized by

Kubernetes). The best way to think of jsonnet is as super-powered JSON combined with a sane way to do templating. Jsonnet combines all the things you wish you could do with JSON (comments, text blocks, parameters, variables, conditionals, file imports), without any of the things that you hate about golang/Jinja2 templating, and adds features that you didn't even know you needed or wanted (functions, object orientation, mixins). It does all of this in a declarative and hermetic (code as data) way.

Jsonnet is not widely adopted in the Kubernetes community, which is unfortunate, because of all the tools described here, jsonnet is hands down the most powerful configuration tools available and is why several offshoot tools are built on-top of it. More on this later. Explaining what's possible with Jsonnet is a post in and of itself, which is why I encourage you to read how Databricks uses Jsonnet with Kubernetes, and Jsonnet's excellent learning tutorial.

The Good:

Extremely powerful. It's rare to hit a situation which couldn't be expressed in some concise and elegant snippet of jsonnet. With jsonnet, you are constantly finding new ways to maximize re-use and avoid repeating yourself.

The Bad:

It's not YAML. This might just be an issue with unfamiliarity, but most people will experience some level of cognitive load when they're staring at a non-trivial jsonnet file. In the same way that you would need to run helm template to verify your Helm chart is producing what you expect, you will similarly need to run jsonnet --yaml-stream guestbook.jsonnetto verify your jsonnet is correct. The good news is that, unlike golang templating which can produce syntactically incorrect YAML due to some misplaced whitespace, with jsonnet these type of errors are caught during build and the resulting output is guaranteed to be valid JSON/YAML.

Ksonnet (and other jsonnet derivatives)

Ksonnet (wordplay on the language for which it is based upon) was supposed to be the "jsonnet for Kubernetes." It provided an opinionated way to organize your jsonnet manifests into files & directories of "components" and "environments," backed by a CLI to help facilitate management of these files. Ksonnet made a big splash nearly two years ago wh en it was jointly announced by Heptio and B itnami, working in conjunction with Microsoft and B ox, a v eritable who's who of th e Kubernetes ecosystem. Fast forward to today, and

~~Heptio~~ VMware announces that the ksonnet project is now being sunsetted.

So what happened? Simply put, it was too hard to use. When starting with ksonnet, you were actually learning three things all at the same time: 1. the jsonnet language itself. 2. ksonnet's over-engineered concepts (components, prototypes, environments, parts, registries, modules). 3. ksonnet-lib, ksonnet's k8s jsonnet library. And if you were new to Kubernetes (as our dev teams were), make that four. Argo CD started with initial support for ksonnet and as someone who pushed for ksonnet adoption at Intuit, I am sorry to see it go. Despite my own efforts to make ksonnet easier for teams, I witnessed first-hand the continued struggles users faced with the tool.

Aside from ksonnet, there are a fair number of other jsonnet derived tools. These include kubecfg, kapitan, kasane, kr8. I don't have first-hand experience with them, but they are definitely worth a look.Ksonnet (and other jsonnet derivatives)

Replicated Ship

Ship, by replicated is relatively new to the scene, and focuses primarily on the problem of "last-mile customization" of third-party applications. It works by using both Helm and Kustomize to generate manifests. Why would you need to do this, you ask? Sooner or later, you will encounter a situation where a Helm chart is almost what you want, but you still need to tweak it somehow (e.g. add Network Policies, set Pod Affinity, etc…). After reviewing the built-in chart parameters, you realize that the chart doesn't provide an option for what you're trying to do. At this point people usually do one of two things: submit a PR upstream to add yet another parameter in the chart, or dump the contents of helm template into a file and hand-edit the YAML with their desired changes. The problem with the latter is that it's unmaintainable. When the time comes to get the latest from upstream, you can't easily discern or reapply the modifications you made in your fork. Ship solves this by keeping these separate: a tracking reference and staging directory hold the upstream helm chart, alongside your last-mile modifications written as kustomization overlays. Using this technique, the base manifests which you receive from upstream can be updated independently from your local kustomizations.

The Good:

It fills a gap. Ship makes it dead simple for operators to custom tailor a chart without having to a push change upstream. There's even a wonderful UI to help guide you through this process.

The Bad:

Only works for OTS. Ship is only intended to be used with an off-the-shelf, upstream source, which means it does not handle the bespoke application config use case at all.

We shouldn't need Ship. I find it unfortunate that we even need a tool like Ship. This is not a problem with Ship itself, but a commentary about the shortcomings of our current tools. Imagine, for example, if Helm provided a built-in way to apply simple overlays to upstream charts (as an alternative to parameters), we would end up with much simpler charts without the mess of overly parameterized templates. Another scenario is to imagine a world where everyone provided kustomize apps for their projects. If this was prevalent, then users could use kustomize's remote base feature to apply local changes against upstream kustomize apps. But unless either of those things happen, Ship is a tool to bridge that gap.

Helm 3 and Lua Script

I'm quite optimistic about the proposal for Helm 3 and its use of Lua based charts. Unfortunately, this aspect of Helm 3 is one of the least developed, and the maintainers have only just begun writing the underlying Lua VM which will power the rendering engine, so it will be quite some time before we'll have more readable charts. I do hope that they can address the last-mile customization gap, and be more friendly to GitOps style of deployments with the Helm 3 redesign.

Kubernetes configuration management is at an inflection point. With kustomize now readily available at user's fingertips, it is easier than ever to guide users towards an extremely capable configuration management out-of-the-box. But if there's a single takeaway from this discussion, it is that there is no perfect configuration management tool and they tend to come and go as the wind blows. Each tool will have its strengths and weaknesses, so it's important to understand when to use the right one for the job. At this moment, we have a mix of apps defined in kustomize, Helm, ksonnet, all in the same cluster for different reasons. With Argo CD, a guiding principle has been to provide users the most amount of flexibility in this regard, such as facilities to customize the repo server, and supporting the ability to execute custom commands to generate manifests.
The state of Kubernetes config management has never been more exciting (as exciting as writing

text to generate more text can be :-). Kustomize's merge into kubectl changes the game entirely. Ksonnet's exit from the market is a sign of the space maturing. Jsonnet will always have a place for the power users. And while Helm has lost some community sentiment as of late with Tiller security concerns and template complexity, it does have a wildcard up its sleeve with Helm 3 and upcoming Lua charts. At the very least, Kubernetes configuration management is a rapidly evolving space which affects all Kubernetes users in some shape or form and everyone should have a vested interest in how things shape up in the years to come.

Chapter 3: An Introduction To Helm, The Package Manager For Kubernetes

Deploying applications to Kubernetes – the powerful and popular container-orchestration system – can be complex. Setting up a single application can involve creating multiple interdependent Kubernetes resources – such as pods, services, deployments, and replicasets – each requiring you to write a detailed YAML manifest file.

Helm is a package manager for Kubernetes that allows developers and operators to more easily package, configure, and deploy applications and services onto Kubernetes clusters.

Helm is now an official Kubernetes project and is part of the Cloud Native Computing Foundation, a non-profit that supports open source projects in and around the Kubernetes ecosystem.

In this book we will give an overview of Helm and the various abstractions it uses to simplify deploying applications to Kubernetes. If you are new to Kubernetes, it may be helpful to read An Introduction to Kubernetes first to familiarize yourself with the basics concepts.

An Overview of Helm

Most every programming language and operating system has its own package manager to help with the installation and maintenance of software. Helm provides the same basic feature set as many of the package managers you may already be familiar with, such as Debian's apt, or Python's pip.

Helm can:

- Install software.
- Automatically install software dependencies.
- Upgrade software.
- Configure software deployments.
- Fetch software packages from repositories.

Helm provides this functionality through the following components:

- A command line tool, helm, which provides the user interface to all Helm functionality.
- A companion server component, tiller, that runs on your Kubernetes cluster, listens for commands from helm, and handles the configuration and deployment of software releases on the cluster.
- The Helm packaging format, called charts.
- An official curated charts repository with prepackaged charts for popular open-source software projects.

We'll investigate the charts format in more detail next.

Charts

Helm packages are called charts, and they consist of a few YAML configuration files and some templates that are rendered into Kubernetes manifest files. Here is the basic directory structure of a chart:
These directories and files have the following functions:

- charts/: Manually managed chart dependencies can be placed in this directory, though it is typically better to use requirements.yaml to dynamically link dependencies.

- templates/: This directory contains template files that are combined with configuration values (from values.yaml and the command line) and rendered into Kubernetes manifests. The templates use the Go programming language's template format.
- Chart.yaml: A YAML file with metadata about the chart, such as chart name and version, maintainer information, a relevant website, and search keywords.
- LICENSE: A plaintext license for the chart.
- README.md: A readme file with information for users of the chart.
- requirements.yaml: A YAML file that lists the chart's dependencies.
- values.yaml: A YAML file of default configuration values for the chart.

The helm command can install a chart from a local directory, or from a .tar.gz packaged version of this directory structure. These packaged charts can also be automatically downloaded and installed from chart repositories or repos.

We'll look at chart repositories next.

Chart Repositories

A Helm chart repo is a simple HTTP site that serves an index.yaml file and .tar.gz packaged charts. The helm command has subcommands available to help package charts and create the required index.yaml file. These files can be served by any web server, object storage service, or a static site host such as GitHub Pages.

Helm comes preconfigured with a default chart repository, referred to as stable. This repo points to a Google Storage bucket at https://kubernetes-charts.storage.googleapis.com. The source for the stable repo can be found in the helm/charts Git repository on GitHub.

Alternate repos can be added with the helm repo add command. Some popular alternate repositories are:

- The official incubator repo that contains charts that are not yet ready for stable. Instructions for using incubator can be found on the official Helm charts GitHub page.
- Bitnami Helm Charts which provide some charts that aren't covered in the official stable repo.

- Whether you're installing a chart you've developed locally, or one from a repo, you'll need to configure it for your particular setup. We'll look into configs next.

Chart Configuration

A chart usually comes with default configuration values in its values.yaml file. Some applications may be fully deployable with default values, but you'll typically need to override some of the configuration to meet your needs.

The values that are exposed for configuration are determined by the author of the chart. Some are used to configure Kubernetes primitives, and some may be passed through to the underlying container to configure the application itself.

These are options to configure a Kubernetes Service resource. You can use helm inspect values chart-name to dump all of the available configuration values for a chart.

These values can be overridden by writing your own YAML file and using it when running helm install, or by setting options individually on the command line with the --set flag. You only need to specify those values that you want to change from the defaults.

A Helm chart deployed with a particular configuration is called a release. We will talk about releases next.

Releases

During the installation of a chart, Helm combines the chart's templates with the configuration specified by the user and the defaults in value.yaml. These are rendered into Kubernetes manifests that are then deployed via the Kubernetes API. This creates a release, a specific configuration and deployment of a particular chart.

This concept of releases is important, because you may want to deploy the same application more than once on a cluster. For instance, you may need multiple MySQL servers with different configurations.

You also will probably want to upgrade different instances of a chart individually. Perhaps one application is ready for an updated MySQL server but another is not. With Helm, you upgrade each release individually.

You might upgrade a release because its chart has been updated, or because you want to update the release's configuration. Either way, each upgrade will create a new revision of a release, and Helm will allow you to easily roll back to previous revisions in case there's an issue.

Creating Charts

If you can't find an existing chart for the software you are deploying, you may want to create your own. Helm can output the scaffold of a chart directory with helm create chart-name. This will create a folder with the files and directories we discussed in the Charts section above.
From there, you'll want to fill out your chart's metadata in Chart.yaml and put your Kubernetes manifest files into the templates directory. You'll then need to extract relevant configuration variables out of your manifests and into values.yaml, then include them back into your manifest templates using the templating system.

The helm command has many subcommands available to help you test, package, and serve your charts. For more information, please read the official Helm documentation on developing charts.

KUBERNETES HELM

Kubernetes HelmKubernetes Helm is a package manager for Kubernetes, analogous to Yum or Apt. It makes it possible to organize Kubernetes objects in a packaged application that anyone can download and install in one click, or configure to their specific needs. In Helm, these packages are called charts (similar to debs or rpms).

When a user installs a Helm chart, Helm deploys a Kubernetes cluster in the background, as specified in the chart's configuration.

Helm is organized around several key concepts:

- A chart is a package of pre-configured Kubernetes resources
- A release is a specific instance of a chart which has been deployed to the cluster using Helm
- A repository is a group of published charts which can be made available to others

What Does Kubernetes Helm Solve?

Kubernetes is known as a complex platform with a steep learning curve. Kubernetes Helm helps make Kubernetes easier and faster to use:

- Improves productivity - instead of spending time on deploying test environments to test their Kubernetes clusters, developers can deploy a pre-tested app via a Helm chart and focus on developing their applications.
- Existing Helm Charts - allow developers to get a working database, big data platform, CMS, etc. deployed for their application with one click. Developers can modify existing charts or create their own to automate dev, test or production processes.

- Easier to start with Kubernetes - it can be difficult to get started with Kubernetes and learn how to deploy production-grade applications. Helm provides one click deployment of apps, making it much easier to get started and deploy your first app, even if you don't have extensive container experience.
- Reduced complexity - deployment of Kubernetes-orchestrated apps can be extremely complex. Using incorrect values in configuration files or failing to roll out apps correctly from YAML templates can break deployments. Helm Charts allow the community to preconfigure applications, defining values that are fixed and others that are configurable with sensible defaults, providing a consistent interface for changing configuration. This dramatically reduces complexity, and eliminates deployment errors by locking out incorrect configurations.
- Production ready - running Kubernetes in production with all its components (pods, namespaces, deployments, etc.) is difficult and prone to error. With a tested, stable Helm chart, users can deploy to production with confidence, and reduce the complexity of maintaining a Kubernetes App Catalog.
- No duplicated effort - once a developer has created a chart, tested and stabilized it once, it can be reused across multiple groups in an organization and outside it. Previously, it was much more difficult (but not impossible) to share

Kubernetes applications and replicate them between environments.

Kubernetes Helm Architecture

Helm consists of two main components:

- Helm Client - allows developers to create new charts, manage chart repositories, and interact with the tiller server.
- Tiller Server - runs inside the Kubernetes cluster. Interacts with Helm client, and translates chart definitions and configuration to Kubernetes API commands. Tiller combines a chart and its configuration to build a release. Tiller is also responsible for upgrading charts, or uninstalling and deleting them from the Kubernetes cluster.

- After Helm is installed, the helm init command installs the Tiller server to your running Kubernetes cluster. It is then possible to search for charts and install them to the cluster.

Chart Templates and Values

A Chart template is a mechanism by which the creator of the chart can define variables that users can modify when installing the chart. Those variables are called values, and the chart must define reasonable defaults for all values to ensure the chart installs correctly out of the box.

Chart templates are written in Go. All template files are stored in a chart's templates/ folder. When Helm accesses a chart, every file in that directory is rendered via the template engine.

To provide values for a template in a specific chart:

- You can provide a file called values.yaml inside of a chart, which contains default values.
- Chart users may supply a YAML file that contains values. This can be provided in the helm install command. User-provided values override the default values in the values.yaml file.

Hooks

Helm provides a hook mechanism, which allows a developer to intervene at specific points in a release's life cycle. The available hooks are:

- pre-install: after templates are rendered, but before resources created in Kubernetes.
- post-install: after all resources are loaded
- pre-delete: on deletion request before any resources are deleted
- post-delete: on a deletion request after all of the resources have been deleted
- pre-upgrade: on an upgrade request after templates are rendered, before any resources are loaded

- post-upgrade: on an upgrade after all resources have been upgraded
- pre-rollback: on a rollback after templates are rendered, but before any resources have been rolled back
- post-rollback: on a rollback request after all resources have been modified

Technically, hooks are Kubernetes manifest files with special annotations in the metadata section. They are template files, so you can use all the regular template features. Here is an example of a job declared to be run on post-install:

Helm Repositories

A chart repository is a server that houses packaged charts. Any HTTP server that can serve YAML files and tar files can be used as a repository server. Helm does not provide tools for uploading charts to remote repository servers.

A repository has a special file called index.yaml that lists all the packages, together with data that allows retrieving and verifying those packages.

On the client side, repositories are managed with the helm repo commands.

Chapter 4: How To Create A Kubernetes Cluster Using Kubeadm

Goals

Your cluster will include the following physical resources:

One master node

The master node (a node in Kubernetes refers to a server) is responsible for managing the state of the cluster. It runs Etcd, which stores cluster data among components that schedule workloads to worker nodes.

Two worker nodes

Worker nodes are the servers where your workloads (i.e. containerized applications and services) will run. A worker will continue to run your workload once they're assigned to it, even if the master goes down once scheduling is complete. A cluster's capacity can be increased by adding workers.

After completing this guide, you will have a cluster ready to run containerized applications, provided that the servers in the cluster have sufficient CPU and RAM resources for your applications to consume. Almost any traditional Unix application including web applications, databases, daemons, and command line tools can be containerized and made to run on the cluster. The cluster itself will consume around 300-500MB of memory and 10% of CPU on each node.

Once the cluster is set up, you will deploy the web server Nginx to it to ensure that it is running workloads correctly.

Prerequisites

- An SSH key pair on your local Linux/macOS/BSD machine. If you haven't used SSH keys before, you can learn how to set them up by following this explanation of how to set up SSH keys on your local machine.

- Three servers running Ubuntu 18.04 with at least 1GB RAM. You should be able to SSH into each server as the root user with your SSH key pair.

- Ansible installed on your local machine. If you're running Ubuntu 18.04 as your OS, follow the "Step 1 - Installing Ansible" section in How to Install and Configure Ansible on Ubuntu 18.04 to install Ansible. For installation instructions on other platforms like macOS or CentOS, follow the official Ansible installation documentation.

- Familiarity with Ansible playbooks. For review, check out Configuration Management 101: Writing Ansible Playbooks.

- Knowledge of how to launch a container from a Docker image. Look at "Step 5 — Running a Docker Container" in How To Install and Use Docker on Ubuntu 18.04 if you need a refresher.

Step 1 — Setting Up the Workspace Directory and Ansible Inventory File

In this section, you will create a directory on your local machine that will serve as your workspace. You will configure Ansible locally so that it can communicate with and execute commands on your remote servers. Once that's done, you will create a hosts file containing inventory information such as the IP addresses of your servers and the groups that each server belongs to.

Out of your three servers, one will be the master with an IP displayed as master_ip. The other two servers will be workers and will have the IPs worker_1_ip and worker_2_ip.

Create a directory named ~/kube-cluster in the home directory of your local machine and cd into it:

This directory will be your workspace for the rest of the tutorial and will contain all of your Ansible playbooks. It will also be the directory inside which you will run all local commands.

Create a file named ~/kube-cluster/hosts using nano or your favorite text editor:

Add the following text to the file, which will specify information about the logical structure of your cluster:

You may recall that inventory files in Ansible are used to specify server information such as IP addresses, remote users, and groupings of servers to target as a single unit for executing commands. ~/kube-cluster/hosts will be your inventory file and you've added two Ansible groups (masters and workers) to it specifying the logical structure of your cluster.

In the masters group, there is a server entry named "master" that lists the master node's IP (master_ip) and specifies that Ansible should run remote commands as the root user.

Similarly, in the workers group, there are two entries for the worker servers (worker_1_ip and worker_2_ip) that also specify the ansible_user as root.
The last line of the file tells Ansible to use the remote servers' Python 3 interpreters for its management operations.

Save and close the file after you've added the text.

Having set up the server inventory with groups, let's move on to installing operating system level dependencies and creating configuration settings.

Step 2 — Creating a Non-Root User on All Remote Servers

In this section you will create a non-root user with sudo privileges on all servers so that you can SSH into them manually as an unprivileged user. This can be useful if, for example, you would like to see system information with commands such as top/htop, view a list of running containers, or change configuration files owned by root. These operations are routinely performed during the maintenance of a cluster, and using a non-root user for such tasks minimizes the risk of modifying or deleting important files or unintentionally performing other dangerous operations.

Create a file named ~/kube-cluster/initial.yml in the workspace:

Next, add the following play to the file to create a non-root user with sudo privileges on all of the servers. A play in Ansible is a collection of steps to be performed that target specific servers and groups.
Here's a breakdown of what this playbook does:

- Creates the non-root user ubuntu.

- Configures the sudoers file to allow the ubuntu user to run sudo commands without a password prompt.

- Adds the public key in your local machine (usually ~/.ssh/id_rsa.pub) to the remote ubuntu user's authorized key list. This will allow you to SSH into each server as the ubuntu user.

Save and close the file after you've added the text.

Next, execute the playbook by locally running:

Step 3 — Installing Kubernetetes' Dependencies

In this section, you will install the operating-system-level packages required by Kubernetes with Ubuntu's package manager. These packages are:

- Docker - a container runtime. It is the component that runs your containers. Support for other runtimes such as rkt is under active development in Kubernetes.

- kubeadm - a CLI tool that will install and configure the various components of a cluster in a standard way.

- kubelet - a system service/program that runs on all nodes and handles node-level operations.
- kubectl - a CLI tool used for issuing commands to the cluster through its API Server.

Create a file named ~/kube-cluster/kube-dependencies.yml in the workspace:

The first play in the playbook does the following:

- Installs Docker, the container runtime.
- Installs apt-transport-https, allowing you to add external HTTPS sources to your APT sources list.

- Adds the Kubernetes APT repository's apt-key for key verification.

- Adds the Kubernetes APT repository to your remote servers' APT sources list.

- Installs kubelet and kubeadm.

The second play consists of a single task that installs kubectl on your master node.

After execution, Docker, kubeadm, and kubelet will be installed on all of the remote servers. kubectl is not a required component and is only needed for executing cluster commands. Installing it only on the master node makes sense in this context, since you will run kubectl commands only from the master. Note, however, that kubectl commands can be run from any of the worker nodes or from any machine where it can be installed and configured to point to a cluster.

All system dependencies are now installed. Let's set up the master node and initialize the cluster.

Step 4 — Setting Up the Master Node

In this section, you will set up the master node. Before creating any playbooks, however, it's worth covering a few concepts such as Pods and Pod Network Plugins, since your cluster will include both.

A pod is an atomic unit that runs one or more containers. These containers share resources such as file volumes and network interfaces in common. Pods are the basic unit of scheduling in Kubernetes: all containers in a pod are guaranteed to run on the same node that the pod is scheduled on.

Each pod has its own IP address, and a pod on one node should be able to access a pod on another node using the pod's IP. Containers on a single node can communicate easily through a local interface. Communication between pods is more complicated, however, and requires a separate networking component that can transparently route traffic from a pod on one node to a pod on another.

This functionality is provided by pod network plugins. For this cluster, you will use Flannel, a stable and performant option.

Create an Ansible playbook named master.yml on your local machine:

Here's a breakdown of this play:

- The first task initializes the cluster by running kubeadm init. Passing the argument --pod-network-cidr=10.244.0.0/16 specifies the private subnet that the pod IPs will be assigned from. Flannel uses the above subnet by default; we're telling kubeadm to use the same subnet.

- The second task creates a .kube directory at /home/ubuntu. This directory will hold configuration information such as the admin key files, which are required to connect to the cluster, and the cluster's API address.

- The third task copies the /etc/kubernetes/admin.conf file that was generated from kubeadm init to your non-root user's home directory. This will allow you to use kubectl to access the newly-created cluster.

- The last task runs kubectl apply to install Flannel. kubectl apply -f descriptor.[yml|json] is the syntax for telling kubectl to create the objects described in the descriptor.[yml|json] file. The kube-flannel.yml file contains the descriptions of objects required for setting up Flannel in the cluster.

Save and close the file when you are finished.

The output states that the master node has completed all initialization tasks and is in a Ready state from which it can start accepting worker nodes and executing tasks sent to the API Server. You can now add the workers from your local machine.

Step 5 — Setting Up the Worker Nodes

Adding workers to the cluster involves executing a single command on each. This command includes the necessary cluster information, such as the IP address and port of the master's API Server, and a secure token. Only nodes that pass in the secure token will be able join the cluster.

Navigate back to your workspace and create a playbook named workers.yml:

Here's what the playbook does:

- The first play gets the join command that needs to be run on the worker nodes. This command will be in the following format:kubeadm join --token <token> <master-ip>:<master-port> --discovery-token-ca-cert-hash sha256:<hash>. Once it gets the actual command with the proper token and hash values, the task sets it as a fact so that the next play will be able to access that info.

- The second play has a single task that runs the join command on all worker nodes. On completion of this task, the two worker nodes will be part of the cluster.

Save and close the file when you are finished.

Execute the playbook by locally running:

With the addition of the worker nodes, your cluster is now fully set up and functional, with workers ready to run workloads. Before scheduling applications, let's verify that the cluster is working as intended.

Step 6 — Verifying the Cluster

A cluster can sometimes fail during setup because a node is down or network connectivity between the master and worker is not working correctly. Let's verify the cluster and ensure that the nodes are operating correctly.

You will need to check the current state of the cluster from the master node to ensure that the nodes are ready. If you disconnected from the master node, you can SSH back into it with the following command:

If all of your nodes have the value Ready for STATUS, it means that they're part of the cluster and ready to run workloads.

If, however, a few of the nodes have NotReady as the STATUS, it could mean that the worker nodes haven't finished their setup yet. Wait for around five to ten minutes before re-running kubectl get nodes and inspecting the new output. If a few nodes still have NotReady as the status, you might have to verify and re-run the commands in the previous steps.

Now that your cluster is verified successfully, let's schedule an example Nginx application on the cluster.

Step 7 — Running An Application on the Cluster

You can now deploy any containerized application to your cluster. To keep things familiar, let's deploy Nginx using Deployments and Services to see how this application can be deployed to the cluster. You can use the commands below for other containerized applications as well, provided you change the Docker image name and any relevant flags (such as ports and volumes).

Still within the master node, execute the following command to create a deployment named nginx:

A deployment is a type of Kubernetes object that ensures there's always a specified number of pods running based on a defined template, even if the pod crashes during the cluster's lifetime. The above deployment will create a pod with one container from the Docker registry's Nginx Docker Image.

Next, run the following command to create a service named nginx that will expose the app publicly. It will do so through a NodePort, a scheme that will make the pod accessible through an arbitrary port opened on each node of the cluster:

Services are another type of Kubernetes object that expose cluster internal services to clients, both internal and external. They are also capable of load balancing requests to multiple pods, and are an integral component in Kubernetes, frequently interacting with other components.

Run the following command:

From the third line of the above output, you can retrieve the port that Nginx is running on. Kubernetes will assign a random port that is greater than 30000 automatically, while ensuring that the port is not already bound by another service.
To test that everything is working, visit http://worker_1_ip:nginx_port or http://worker_2_ip:nginx_port through a browser on your local machine. You will see Nginx's familiar welcome page.

If you would like to remove the Nginx application, first delete the nginx service from the master node:

Chapter 5: Deploy, Scale And Upgrade An Application On Kubernetes With Helm

Containers have revolutionized application development and delivery on account of their ease of use, portability and consistency. And when it comes to automatically deploying and managing containers in the cloud (public, private or hybrid), one of the most popular options today is Kubernetes.

Kubernetes is an open source project designed specifically for container orchestration. Kubernetes offers a number of key features, including multiple storage APIs, container health checks, manual or automatic scaling, rolling upgrades and service discovery. Applications can be installed to a Kubernetes cluster via Helm charts, which provide streamlined package management functions.

If you're new to Kubernetes and Helm charts, one of the easiest ways to discover their capabilities is with Bitnami. Bitnami offers a number of stable, production-ready Helm charts to deploy popular software applications, such as WordPress, Magento, Redmine and many more, in a Kubernetes cluster. Or, if you're developing a custom application, it's also possible to use

Bitnami's Helm charts to package and deploy it for Kubernetes.

This guide walks you through the process of bootstrapping an example MongoDB, Express, Angular and Node.js (MEAN) application on a Kubernetes cluster. It uses a custom Helm chart to create a Node.js and MongoDB environment and then clone and deploy a MEAN application from a public Github repository into that environment. Once the application is deployed and working, it also explores some of Kubernetes' most interesting features: cluster scaling, load-balancing, and rolling updates.

Assumptions and Prerequisites

This guide focuses on deploying an example MEAN application in a Kubernetes cluster running on either Google Container Engine (GKE) or Minikube. The example application is a single-page Node.js and Mongo-DB to-do application available on Github.

This guide makes the following assumptions:

- You have a Kubernetes 1.5.0 (or later) cluster.
- You have kubectl installed and configured to work with your Kubernetes cluster.
- You have git installed and configured.

• You have a basic understanding of how containers work.

Step 1: Validate the Kubernetes cluster
First, ensure that you are able to connect to your cluster with kubectl cluster-info. This command is also a good way to get the IP address of your cluster.
Step 2: Install Helm and Tiller

To install Helm, execute these commands:

Step 3: Deploy the example application

The smallest deployable unit in Kubernetes is a "pod". A pod consists of one or more containers which can communicate and share data with each other. Pods make it easy to scale applications: scale up by adding more pods, scale down by removing pods. Learn more about pods.

The Helm chart used in this guide deploys the example to-do application as two pods: one for Node.js and the other for MongoDB. This is considered a best practice because it allows a clear separation of concerns, and it also allows the pods to be scaled independently (you'll see this in the next section).

To deploy the sample application using a Helm chart, follow these steps:

- Clone the Helm chart from Bitnami's Github repository:
- Check for and install missing dependencies with helm dep. The Helm chart used in this example is dependent on the MongoDB chart in the official repository, so the commands below will take care of identifying and installing the missing dependency.
- Lint the chart with helm lint to ensure it has no errors.
- Deploy the Helm chart with helm install. This will produce two pods (one for the Node.js service and the other for the MongoDB service). Pay special attention to the NOTES section of the output, as it contains important information to access the application.

Get the URL for the Node application by executing the commands shown in the output of helm install, or by using helm status my-todo-app and checking the output for the external IP address.

If you deployed the application on GKE, use these commands to obtain the URL for the Node application:

If you deployed the application on Minikube, use these commands instead to obtain the URL for the Node application:

Browse to the specified URL and you should see the sample application running. Here's what it should look like:

To debug and diagnose deployment problems, use kubectl get pods -l app=my-todo-app-mean. If you specified a different release name (or didn't specify one), remember to use the actual release name from your deployment.

To delete and reinstall the Helm chart at any time, use the helm delete command, shown below. The additional --purge option removes the release name from the store so that it can be reused later.

Step 4: Explore Kubernetes and Helm
Scale up (or down)

As more and more users access your application, it becomes necessary to scale up in order to handle the increased load. Conversely, during periods of low demand, it often makes sense to scale down to optimize resource usage.
Kubernetes provides the kubectl scale command to scale the number of pods in a deployment up or down.

A key feature of Kubernetes is that it is a self-healing system: if one or more pods in a Kubernetes cluster are terminated unexpectedly, the cluster will automatically spin up replacements. This ensures that the required number of pods are always running at any given time.

As you can see, this cluster has been scaled up to have 2 Node.js pods. Now, select one of the Node.js pods and simulate a pod failure by deleting it with a command like the one below. Replace the POD-ID placeholder with an actual pod identifier from the output of the kubectl get pods command.

If you keep watching the output of kubectl get pods -w, you will see the state of the new pod change rapidly from “Pending” to “Running”.

Balance traffic between pods

It’s easy enough to spin up two (or more) replicas of the same pod, but how do you route traffic to them? When deploying an application to a Kubernetes cluster in the cloud, you have the option of automatically creating a cloud network load balancer (external to the Kubernetes cluster) to direct traffic between the pods. This load balancer is an example of a Kubernetes Service resource. Learn more about services in Kubernetes.

You’ve already seen a Kubernetes load balancer in action. When deploying the application to GKE

with Helm, the command used the serviceType option to create an external load balancer,
When invoked in this way, Kubernetes will not only create an external load balancer, but will also take care of configuring the load balancer with the internal IP addresses of the pods, setting up firewall rules, and so on. To see details of the load balancer service, use the kubectl describe svc command,

Notice the LoadBalancer Ingress field, which specifies the IP address of the load balancer, and the Endpoints field, which specifies the internal IP addresses of the three Node.js pods in use. Similarly, the Port field specifies the port that the load balancer will listen to for connections (in this case, 80, the standard Web server port) and the NodePort field specifies the port on the internal cluster node that the pod is using to expose the service.

Obviously, this doesn't work quite the same way on a Minikube cluster running locally. Look back at the Minikube deployment and you'll see that the serviceType option was set to NodePort. This exposes the service on a specific port on every node in the cluster.

The main difference here is that instead of an external network load balancer service, Kubernetes creates a service that listens on each node for incoming requests and directs it to the static open port on each endpoint.

Perform rolling updates (and rollbacks)

Rolling updates and rollbacks are important benefits of deploying applications into a Kubernetes cluster. With rolling updates, devops teams can perform zero-downtime application upgrades, which is an important consideration for production environments. By the same token, Kubernetes also supports rollbacks, which enable easy reversal to a previous version of an application without a service outage.

By now, you should have a good idea of how some of the key features available in Kubernetes, such as scaling and automatic load balancing, work. You should also have an appreciation for how Helm charts make it easier to perform common actions in a Kubernetes deployment, including installing, upgrading and rolling back applications.

Chapter 6: First Steps With Kubernetes

Establishing a complete, multi-knot Kubernetes cluster is not an easy task, especially if you don't know about Linux and network administration. Proper deployment of Kubernetes spans across several physical and virtual machines and includes an adequate network setup to allow all containers in the cluster to communicate.

You can install Kubernetes on your desktop, on the network of your organization or virtual machinery supplied by cloud providers (Google Compute Engine, Amazon EC2, Microsoft Azure, etc.). Instead, most cloud providers also provide managed Kubernetes services that save you from deployment and management problems. Here is a brief overview of the service of the largest cloud providers:

Google offers GKE - Google Kubernetes Engine,
Amazon has EKS - Amazon Elastic Kubernetes Service,
Microsoft has AKS – Azure Kubernetes Service,
IBM has IBM Cloud Kubernetes Service,

Alibaba provides the Alibaba Cloud Container Service.

Installing and managing Kubernetes is much harder than just using them, mainly if you know their architecture and operation intimately. This is why we will begin with the easiest ways to get a working Kubernetes cluster. You can learn different ways to run a Kubernetes cluster with only one node on your local computer and how to use a Google Kubernetes Engine (GKE) hosted cluster.

A third option is given in Appendix B, which includes the installation of a cluster using a kubeadm tool and shows you how to set up a three-node Kubernetes cluster using virtual machines. But you might want to try this only after you learn how to use Kubernetes. There are also many other choices, but they are beyond the reach of this book. See the kubernetes.io website for more information.

If someone else has given you access to an existing cluster, you can skip this section to Section 3.2, where you learn how to communicate with clusters in Kubernetes.

Using the built-in Kubernetes cluster in Docker Desktop

You probably have installed Docker Desktop if you use macOS or Windows to run the exercises in the previous chapter. It includes a Kubernetes Cluster with a single node that can be enabled via its Settings dialog. That can be the easiest way for you to begin your trip to Kubernetes, but note that Kubernetes may not be as recent as when you use the alternative options mentioned in the following sections.

Enabling Kubernetes in Docker Desktop

When Docker Desktop is mounted on your computer, you can open the Settings dialog box by clicking the whale icon on the system tray. Click on the Kubernetes tab and make sure the checkbox Allow Kubernetes is selected. The components that make up the Control Plane run as Docker containers, but when you invoke the Docker ps command, they do not appear on the list of running containers.

Visualizing the system

See the following figure for an overview of the various components of the Kubernetes cluster in the Docker Desktop.

Docker Desktop builds a virtual Linux computer with the Docker Daemon and all containers. The VM also operates the Kubelet–the node manager for Kubernetes. The Control Plane components operate in containers along with all applications that you deploy.

You don't need to log in to the VM to list the running containers since the CLI docker available in your host operating system displays them.

Exploring the Virtual Machine from the inside

Docker Desktop does not provide a command to connect to the VM at the time of writing if you want to explore it from within. Nevertheless, you can use a special container to run a remote shell that is almost similar to SSH for accessing a remote server using VM namespaces.

Running a local cluster using Minikube

The flag-it controls the collaborative mode of the container, and the flag —rm ensures that the container is removed once it stops.

Another way to create a Kubernetes cluster is to use Minikube, a Kubernetes tool. The Kubernetes version used by Minikube is typically newer than the version used by Docker Desktop. The cluster has one node and is designed for the local testing and development of Kubernetes. Usually, it runs on Kubernetes in a Linux VM, but it can also deploy Kubernetes directly on your host OS via Docker if your machine is Linux based.

You can install it on macOS using Brew Package Manager, download an installer from Windows and download a.deb or.rpm package on Ubuntu, or you can download a binary file and make it executable with the following order.

$ minikube start
minikube v1.6.2 on Fedora 30
Selecting 'virtualbox' driver from user configuration (alternates: [none])
Downloading VM boot image ...
Creating virtualbox VM (CPUs=2, Memory=2000MB, Disk=20000MB) ...
Preparing Kubernetes v1.17.0 on Docker '19.03.5' ...

Downloading kubelet v1.17.0
Downloading kubeadm v1.17.0
Pulling images ...
Launching Kubernetes ...
Waiting for cluster to come online ...
Done! kubectl is now configured to use "minikube"
If no choice is used by —VM-driver to build the cluster, the Control Plane components run in a VM container or directly in your host OS. The Kubelet works directly on the VM or the operating system of your server. It runs the applications that you use through the Docker Daemon in the cluster.
Like Minikube, kind is a single executable binary file. For installation, refer to the https:/kind.sigs.k8s.io/docs/user/quick-start/ installation instructions.

This makes the perfect tool for development and testing since everything works locally, and you can easily debug running processes out of the container. I would instead use this approach in developing applications on Kubernetes because it enables me to do awesome things like running network traffic analysis tools such as Wireshark or even my web browser inside containers running my applications. I use a nsenter tool that allows me to run certain tools on the container's network or other namespaces.

Chapter 7: Кuвernетes Governance Producтion

What is Governance?

Governance refers to a set of rules codified as policies to minimize risk, cost control, and drive performance, openness, and environmental accountability. The governance policies may represent both external and compliance requirements and internal security, access to resources, cost control, and acceleration deployment conventions.

Kubernetes' mission-critical workloads in production involve broad and flexible management and operational system that can help managers gain insight and control over these dynamic environments.

The subject of Cuban Governance consists of three sections: security and access control, cost management, and acceleration of deployment. We will discuss best practices for protection and access control and cost management in this chapter.

Security and Access Control

Authentication and authorization are the primary access control principles. Together, they help companies to create a security perimeter around its IT infrastructure, identify open users and processes, and monitor the use of resources.

In Kubernetes, there are two ways to authenticate or classify requests: either as user accounts assigned to teammates or as service accounts for individual processes. When applications are authenticated, Kubernetes resources are available. This process is known as permission.
Kubernetes also allows requests after authentication and authorization to move through an external filter. This group of filters is called input controllers. Admission controllers allow Kubernetes managers to monitor their Kubernetes environments more in granular terms.
Let us now outline Cubans ' best practices in the security and access control sense.
Kubernetes Governance Best Practices: Security and Access Control

Enabled at least two Authentication Methods?
Kubernetes recommends at least two methods of authentication; one for each user account and one for each service account. The suggested way to authenticate service accounts is via tokens. Service tokens are automatically activated.
Allow OpenID Connect or X509 user account authentication client certificates. Authentication of the User Certificate X509 may be enabled by forwarding the —client-ca-file=/mydirectory / ca.crt to the API server. Complete instructions to allow OpenID Connect is provided here.

After the authentication methods are allowed, ensure that static token-based authentication is also disabled. You can do this by removing the flag —token-auth-file= FILENAME from the pod spec API folder.

Disabled Anonymous Authentication?

Versions 1.6 and later in Kubernetes are the default for anonymous authentication. A system: anonymous username and a system: unauthenticated category are allocated to requests not refused by other authentication methods. A best practice for authentication is, therefore, to flag —anonymous-auth= false to the API server.

Public requests for Kubelet should also be disallowed. You can do that by editing the configuration or service files of Kubelet.

Allowing RBAC will also reduce the danger of unauthorized access because, before granting access to resources, RBAC enables anonymous requests be expressly enabled. RBAC can be turned on by running the —authorization-mode= RBAC API command.

Disabled Unauthenticated Access to the API server?

On two ports, LocalHost port, and Secure Port, the Kubernetes API Server can handle requests. The Localhost port is equipped with the API for testing and other master components. Localhost port requests bypass authentication and permission modules.

A best practice is to set the —insecure-port flag to 0 to avoid unauthenticated access to the master node and delete the —insecure-bind-address flag from the API server manifestation.
The —secure-port flag is omitted from the API server spec. This ensures that all protected port requests are authenticated and permitted.
Using User-Access Best Practices for Service Account Tokens?
The tokens used to authenticate service accounts are secretly saved. Such secrets can be used as service accounts by malicious actors. Therefore, it is a good practice to observe best practices for user access and the less fortunate approach when reading such secrets.

Configured Master Node communication?
The API server interacts with each node and any pods, nodes, or services in Kubelet. Default connections to Kubelet do not check the API server. For the link to run securely on untrusted paths and to prevent harmful attacks, the best practice is to supply the API server with a root certificate flag. It helps the API server to validate the service certificate of the Kubelet.
Alternately, using SSH tunneling between the API server and Kubelet and the API server and any nodes, pods, or facilities.

Enabled RBAC?

Kubernetes RBAC provides administrators with the configuration and control of access to and activity on the infrastructure of Kubernetes.

Kubernetes acknowledges that they follow best practices when setting up an RBAC policy. The concept of least privilege is a good thing, and the number of permissions is limited.

Admins must, however, make sure that they decide between a broad or fine-grained RBAC approach. Both have advantages and inconveniences; fine-grained roles and position bindings offer smaller licenses and access but are subject to higher overhead management. Broader tasks and functions are easier to manage but have a more extensive allowance footprint.

The optimum design will most often lie somewhere between the two configurations and will depend on the unique team structure and organizational application design.

Cluster roles allow access and permission across all namespaces for the entire cluster. Therefore, Kubernetes must be vigilant when granting it to users or user groups.

RBAC can be enabled with the —authorization-mode= RBAC flag to start the API server.

Disabled Default Service Account?

The default service account is automatically assigned to all newly created pods and containers without a service account. The default service

account has a vast spectrum of cluster permissions and should be disabled.
This can be achieved by setting autountServiceAccountToken: false on the service.

Configured Access to Etcd clusters?
Connection to Etcd is the same as the root connection in Kubernetes. Therefore, a best practice is to restrict access to etcd only from the API server and the nodes that allow that access. This is a full description of limiting access to and the API server access to the cluster.

Enabled Audit Policy?
The audit by Kubernetes allows us to collect documents performed by individual users, administrators, or other system components for authentication, authorizing, and login activities. Enhanced auditing with event validation, external system integration, and audit policy was implemented in Version 1.7 and 1.8. The audit policy sets out guidelines for the activities to be registered.
Default Advanced Audit is available. The best practice is to pass the "-audit-policy-file=<audit-policy.УAML >" flag to the API server to ensure that incidents are logged.
Version 1.8 also includes the audit policy file to provide the type, version, and a minimum of one rule.

Configured Service Account Permissions?

Kubernetes role bindings allow a collection of permissions to be assigned to individual subjects specified in the roles. Sujets can include user accounts, service accounts, or classes.

By default, service accounts outside the Namespace cube structure have no permissions.

A fine-grained and granular authorization process is best practiced by assigning roles to resources created for individual applications. To do so, an account name service must be included in the pod spec specification. Permissions for this service account can then be given with function bindings, such as limiting it to a particular namespace.

Enabled Recommended Admission Controllers?

As mentioned above, admission controllers are a collection of filters through which requests can be filtered. Admission controllers kick in when applications have been approved, authenticated, and granular controls are provided for which applications are permitted to continue.

Kubernetes offers a selection of ready-to-deploy admission controllers. A good practice is bypassing the —enable-admit-plugins=<admission controller name > flag to the API server, to allow such admission controllers.

The following admission control units have been suggested for Kubernetes v. 1.10: NamespaceLifecycle, LimitRanger,

ServiceAccount, DefaultStorageClass, DefaultTolerationSeconds, MutatingAdmissionWebhook, ValidatingAdmissionWEbhook, Priority, ResourceQuota.

PodSecurityPolicy

PodSecurityPolicy admission controller allows Kubernetes to set a set of conditions that pods must meet to be enabled to function. Kube-API server can recognize pod security policy —-enable-admission-plug-ins= PodSecurityPolicy Moreover, policies should be implemented and approved in the PodSecurityPolicy object before allowing this admission controller.

AlwaysPullImages

AlwaysPullImages is an admission controller which ensures that images are always pulled with correct permission and can not be re-used without credentials. This is useful in a multi-tenant environment and guarantees that only users with the appropriate credentials can use photos.

You can allow AlwaysPullImages images with Kube-apiserver —enable-admission-plugins= AlwaysPullImage Here's how to test which admittance controllers were permitted.

Using the Latest Kubernetes Version?

Critical bug fixes and new security features are rolled out daily by Kubernetes. Make sure you update to the latest version to use these features.

Defined Pod Security Policy and Enabled it in the Admission Controller?

Pod security policies specify a series of safety protocols that are important and must be followed to be scheduled. A recommended admission controller is also PodSecurityPolicy. Here's an example of a stringent safety policy on pods. This policy requires all users to run as users who are unprivileged and also avoids a rise in privileges and other restrictive security policies.

You can use —enable-admission-plugins= PodSecurityPolicy to enable the security policy.

Configured Kubernetes Secrets?

Sensitive information about your Kubernetes system should always be stored in a Kubernetes secret object such as a password, token, or key. You can see a list of the secrets that have already been developed using:

Enabled Data Encryption at Rest?

Encrypting data at rest is another best practice for defense. With Kubernetes, one of these four providers can encrypt data: AES-CBC, secret box, aesgcm, or km.

Encryption can be allowed through the Kube-apiserver method by passing the —encryption-provider-config flag.

Kubectl receipt of Secret —all-namespaces-o JSON kubectl substitute -f –This will also apply server-side encryption to all passwords, to ensure all secrets are encrypted.

Scanned Containers for Security Vulnerabilities?

Another best practice for protection is to check images of your container for known vulnerabilities.

You can do this through open-source tools such as Anchor and Clair to detect and mitigate common vulnerabilities and exposures.

Configured Security Context for Pods, Containers and Volumes?

The protection context defines the configuration of privilege and access control for pods and containers. Pod safety context can be specified by the inclusion in the pod specification of the security context sector. Once a security background has been set for a pod, it propagates automatically to all containers in the package.

A best practice for a pod safety is to set the functions runAsNonRoot and readOnlyRootFileSystem to true and allowPriviligeEscalation to false. It adds more layers into your containers and Kubernetes and stops privileges from increasing.

Enabled Kubernetes Logging?

Kubernetes logs help you understand both what's going on inside your cluster and diagnose problems and track your operation. Logs are usually written to standard outputs and error streams for containerized applications.

A best practice to set up a separate lifecycle and storage for logs is to manage logs from pods, containers, and nodes. You can do this by introducing a logging system at a cluster level.

Cost Management

Cost management relates to the ongoing process of implementing cost control policies. In the sense of Kubernetes, companies can manage and minimize costs in several ways. These include native Cubans tools for planning and controlling the use and consumption of resources and effective control and optimization of the underlying infrastructure. Below we will identify some best practices for cost control in Kubernetes production environments.

Kubernetes Governance Best Practices: Cost Management

Created Separate Namespaces for Teams?

Namespaces of Kubernetes are virtual partitions of clusters of Kubernetes. It is recommended that individual teams, programs, or customers create separate namespaces. Dividing Cubans into different namespaces serves both security and access control and resource management purposes.

Showing a namespace list: kubectl get namespaces

Or

kubectl get namespaces---show-labels. You can also display a list of all namespaces running inside kubectl namespaces— all-name spaces.

Configured Default Resource Requests and Limits?

A best practice is always to define resource requests and limits when operating with Kubernetes containers. Containers without any cap on their resource consumption will result in resource containment with other containers and unoptimized machine consumption.

A good way to ensure all resource requests and limits are distributed in all containers is to create a LimitRange object for each namespace. The object LimitRange enables you to define default values in the namespace for resource requests and limitations for individual containers. Any container within that namespace, with no explicitly specified request and limit values, is allocated the default values.

Using kubectl to test whether default values were set: define namespace < namespace name >

Configured Minimum and Maximum Resource Limits?

Kubernetes can also add limits to the resource request and limits for individual containers with an Object LimitRange.

Configuring a minimum LimitRange value for a namespace guarantees that each container within that namespace has a value that is greater than the resource request value. The maximum LimitRange value is the limit value for a resource and guarantees that Resource limits do not surpass the maximum amount for individual containers within that namespace.

Using kubectl to check that minimum and maximum resource limits have been set: Describe the namespace < name>

Configured Resource Quotas for Namespaces?

The cumulative resource consumption of all containers within a namespace is also best practice. This can be done with a resource quota set. Resource quotas can be programmed for individual namespaces and provide another device resource consumption management layer.

Defining a namespace resource quota would reduce the total amount of CPU, memory, or store resources that all containers that belong to that namespace will consume.

Use kubectl defines namespace < name> to verify whether resource quotas have been set.

Configured Quotas for other Kubernetes Objects?

Quotas for other Kubernetes objects may also be specified. These include pod quotas limiting the number of pods within the namespace and the Application quotas, limiting the number of API objects (PersistentVolumeClaims, Services, and ReplicaSets). Pod and API quotas are another way to manage the Kubernetes cluster's resource consumption and costs.

Therefore, when new namespaces are formed, Kubernetes administrators can configure both pod and API quotas.

To test if quotas have been set, define the namespace < name> for kubectl.

Configured the Horizontal Pod Auto-scaler?

An alternative way to effectively control Kubernetes consumption of resources is the horizontal pod auto-scaler (HPA). The HPA scales the number of Pods in a Kubernetes (or other controllers) automatically, depending on the use of the CPU or other custom metrics. HPA routinely checks the use of pods by CPU and increases or decreases the number of pods depending on the target CPU usage value. For example, the number of Pod replicas is reduced if the CPU usage is less than the target. If the CPU usage is higher than the target value, the number of Pod replicas will be decreased and increased.

This means Kubernetes pods are no longer killed and do not take up resources that could be used elsewhere.

Configured the Cluster Auto-scaler?

The auto-scaler cluster (CA) allows Kubernetes to increase or reduce the resource footprint of a cluster dynamically. This is achieved by reducing or adding to the number of virtual cloud machines (VMs) in the cluster pool.

The auto-scaler cluster adjusts the number of nodes based on two signals: the number of pending pods and the resource use of the nodes.

When the CA detects any pending pods during its regular checks, it asks the cloud provider for additional nodes. The CA also reduces the cluster and eliminates idle nodes if under-used.

Due to the cost of VMs, reducing the number of nodes supplied in response to consumption signals would result in significant cost reductions.

Have a Plan for Rightsizing Instances?

Multiple VMs (nodes) are clustered into clusters in public cloud Kubernetes. Pods run over these nodes and use their energy.

A best practice is to ensure that the resource footprint of the Kubernetes nodes corresponds to the top of the pods. This is reflected most often in terms of node use. The use of nodes is a measure of the Node's overall resource potential relative to the resources used. A higher purpose, in comparison with efficiency, suggests insufficient use and waste of resources.

A best practice is to track the historical and real-time resource usage of individual nodes and resize them when their use falls below a certain threshold to ensure the optimal use of resources. We only use Prometheus and Grafana to create such a control system.

Configured the Vertical Pod Auto-Scaler to Resize Pods?

The VPA scales up or down pod resources based on specified CPU and memory requests values.

Pod resource requests are not an exact science. There are cases where services are required, and actual usage varies widely. When this occurs, the carbon footprint of a pot well exceeds what is necessary to produce wasted energy.

The VPA helps prevent this by scaling up and down pod resource requirements, depending on the resource consumption of each pod. A recommending VPA portion tracks both current and past resource consumption and offers recommended values for resource requests. Any pods which have not set proper resource requests are destroyed, recreated, and allocated by the updater and the input components to the appropriate resource requests.

Have a Plan for Using Reserved/Spot Instances?

Another best practice when spinning clusters is to ensure a healthy balance of reserved and on-demand instances. The chosen type of instance often depends on demands for workload, e.g., task-critical workloads are usually hosted on-demand or on-demand instances. But these types of instances are much more expensive compared to spot cases where defect sensitive applications are typically favored where some downtime is appropriate.

Numerous open-source tools allow Kubernetes to complement reserved or spot instances on-demand instances, thereby reducing costs. Two such open-source tools are K8s Spot Rescheduler and the K8s Spot Instance Termination Manager.

Tagging all Resources?

Tagging tools are another good practice in monitoring and controlling the costs of

Kubernetes. In business environments where multiple teams which participate in different projects provide resources, some resources are bound to fall under the radar. Such tools continue to add costs even though they are not used. Tagging is an effective strategy to ensure that these resources are monitored and included in a central inventory during their lifecycle. It can also easily identify and delete unused properties.

Chapter 8: Manage Dата In Docкer

Docker has two options for host containers to store files, so that even after the container stops the data persisted: volumes and mounts for binding. You can also use a tmpfs mount if you run Docker on Linux. You can also use a called pipe if you run Docker on Windows.

Continue to read more about these two types of persisting results.

Choose the right type of mount

Regardless of the type of mount, you select, the data from the container looks the same. It is displayed as either a directory or as a file in the filesystem of the container.

A simple way to understand the difference between volumes, binding mounts, and tmpfs mounts is to see where the data reside on the Docker host.

Volumes are stored in part of the Docker-managed host filesystem (/var/lib/docker/volumes) This section of the filesystem should not be changed by non-Docker processes. Volumes are the best way to collect Docker data.

Link mounts can be installed on the host network everywhere. They can even be critical machines or directory files. Non-Docker processes can be

changed at any time on the Docker or Docker containers.
tmpfs mounts are only stored in the memory of the host device and are never written to the operating system filesystem.

More details about mount types

Volumes: Docker produced and managed. You may directly build a volume with the command to create the docker volume, or Docker can create a volume when constructing a container or service.
The volume is stored in a directory on the Docker host when you create a file. This directory is what is placed into a container when you install the volume in a container. This is similar to the way binding mounts work except that volumes are managed by Docker and isolated from the host's core functionality.
A provided volume can be placed simultaneously in multiple containers. If no container is running using a volume, the volume is still available and is not automatically removed from Docker. Unused volumes can be deleted with the prune of the docker array.
It may be called or anonymous when mounting a number. When first loaded into a container, unknown volumes are not given a specific name, so Docker gives them a random name that is guaranteed to be unique within a particular Docker host. In addition to the mark, named and anonymous volumes act in the same way.

Volumes also support the use of volume drivers that allow you to store your data, among other options, on remote servers or cloud providers.

Link mounts: Accessible since Docker's early days. Relative to sizes, binding mounts have limited functionality. When using a link mount, a file or directory is placed into a container on the host computer. The file or directory is referenced on the host machine with its entire path. There is no need for the file or directory on the Docker host already. It is generated on request if it does not exist yet. Bind mounts are very powerful but depend on the filesystem of the host machine, which has a different directory structure. Consider using named volumes, if you develop new Docker applications. You can't use Docker CLI to handle attach mounts directly.

tmpfs mounts: tmpfs mount on the disk, on the Docker host or inside a container is not permanent. It can be used throughout a container's existence to store non-persistent or sensitive information. For example, swarm services internally use tmpfs mounts to install secrets in the containers of a server.

Called pipes: pipe mounting can be used between the Docker host and a container for communication. The common practice is the execution of a third-party tool inside a container and the connection via a pipe to the Docker Engine API.

Both the binding mounts and volumes are placed on the -v or—volume flag in the containers, but for each, the syntax is slightly different. You can use the —tmpfs flag for tmpfs mounts. We suggest the use of the —mount flag for both binding mounts, volumes, and tmpfs mounts in Docker 17.06 and higher, as the syntax is simpler.

Good use cases for volumes

Volumes are the easiest way to collect data in containers and applications in Docker. Some cases use volume: sharing of data between multiple containers. If you do not construct it directly, the first time it is placed in a container, a volume is formed. The amount remains when the container stops or is withdrawn. Multiple containers can either read-write or read-only mount the same volume simultaneously. Volumes are only removed when you remove them directly.

If there is no guarantee that the Docker host has a specified directory or file structure. Volumes allow you to isolate the Docker host configuration from the container execution time.

If you want to store data from your container on a remote server or cloud provider instead of locally.

Volumes are a better choice if you need to back up, restore or transfer data from one host to another. Containers can be halted with the volume and the folder of the volume backed up (for example, /var / lib / docker / volumes/<volume-name >).

Good use cases for bind mounts

You will usually use volumes as far as possible. Link mounts are suitable for the following types of use: sharing host configuration files in containers. This is how Docker supplies DNS resolution to containers by mounting /etc / resolv.conf from the host to every container by default.

Share source code or build objects between a Docker host development environment and a container. For example, you can install a Maven target/directory in a container, and each time you build the Maven project on the Docker host, the container will have access to recovered objects.

If you use Docker for creation this way, your Dockerfile output will directly copy the manufacturing objects into the image instead of depending on a binding mount.

The containers are needed when the file or directory structure of the Docker host is guaranteed to be conformed to the bind mounts.

Good use cases for tmpfs mounts

tmpfs mounts are often used in situations where data are not stored on either the host or the container. This may be for security reasons or the efficiency of the container when a large volume of non-persistent state data is to be written on your application.

Tips for using bind mounts or volumes

☐ If you use bind mounts or volumes, remember:

☐ If you mount an empty volume to the directory of files and directories in the container, these files or directories will be distributed (copied) to the volume. Likewise, an empty volume is generated for you if you start a container and define a volume that does not already exist. This is a good way to collect the data needed by another container.

☐ If an attach mount or non-empty volume is inserted into the directory in a container in which some folders or files are present, the mount obscures these files or directories, just as if you were saving files to / mnt on a Linux host and then mounting a USB drive into /mnt. The USB drive contents would hide/mnt content until the USB drive is unmounted. The blurred files are not deleted or changed, but can not be accessed when binding or volume mounting is mounted.

Chapter 9: Kubernetes Configmaps And Secrets

Everybody requires software to be configured. Specific data bits, such as API keys, tokens, and other passwords, must be checked regularly. For instance, a PHP.ini file or environment variables and flags that alter the logic of an app can be configured for your device.

These references may be tempting to hardcode into your application logic. This may be appropriate in a small, standalone application, but it becomes easily unmanageable in any reasonably large device.

Naturally, we solved this problem. You can use environment variables and configuration files to store this information in a "central location." If you want to change your setup, update it, or replace the environmental component, and you're good to go! Not every location where the data are referenced needs to be hunted.

This problem in the land of containers and microservices is aggravated. Docker allows you to enter environmental variables in the Dockerfile, but what about you in two different containers to reference the same data? When you try to use the host system, what happens when you run on a multi-machine cluster?

Let's take an app with a hardcoded configuration, change it to read from the environment variables, and set up Kubernetes to handle your setup.

Step 1: Using Environment Variables

It's easy to move to environment variables. Most programming languages have a readable way.

This is all it takes! It takes it!

We can now set these environment variables and don't have to access the code of our application

In a Unix system like MacOS or Linux, you can run this command to set the current session environment variables:

```
export LANGUAGE=English
export API_KEY=123–456–789
```

For Windows, you can use this command:

```
setx LANGUAGE “English”
setx API_KEY “123–456–789”
```

You can set the location variables when starting the server as well.

For example, for this Node.js app, you can run:

```
LANGUAGE=Spanish API_KEY=0987654 npm start
```

And these will be exposed to the app.

Step 2: Moving to Docker Environment Variables

You can no longer rely on the environmental variables of the host when you switch to a containerized solution. Every container has its own environment, so it is important to ensure that the container's environment is configured correctly. Fortunately, Docker makes it easy to create containers with baked environmental variables. You may define them with the ENV directive in your Dockerfile.

In the same directory as your code, place the Dockerfile.
Create the container then:
docker build -t envtest .
After creating the container, test it with the following command:
docker run -p 3000:3000 -ti envtest
You can also supersede the location variables when running on the command line:

```
docker run -e LANGUAGE=Spanish -e API_KEY=09876 -p 3000:3000 \
       -ti envtest
```

Step 3: Moving to Kubernetes Environment Variables

Things change again when they switch from Docker to Kubernetes. You may be able to use the same Docker container in multiple deployments or to check A / B with your deployments using the same container in different configurations.
You can define ambient variables directly in your Kubernetes deployment YAML file, just like the Dockerfile. This means that every deployment can have a custom environment.

The important part is the env part of the pod spec. You can define as many variables of the environment as you want. All variables are now defined by Kubernetes!

Step 4: Centralized Configuration with Kubernetes Secrets and ConfigMaps

The lack of environment variables for Docker and Kubernetes is that they are connected to the container or deployment. You have to repair the container or adjust the deployment if you want to alter them. Even worse, you have to repeat the data if you want to use the variable for multiple containers or deployments!

Fortunately, Kubernetes fixes this problem with Secrets and ConfigMaps (for non-confidential data).

The significant difference between Secrets and ConfigMaps is that Secrets with a Base64 encoding are blurred. Secrets for confidential data (as API keys) and ConfigMaps for non-confidential data (like port numbers) may be used in the future, but it's a good practice.

Let's save the API key as a Secret:

kubectl create secret generic apikey --from-literal=API_KEY=123–456

And the language as a ConfigMap:

kubectl create configmap language --from-literal=LANGUAGE=English

You can check that these are created with the following commands:

kubectl get secret

Updating Secrets and ConfigMaps

As mentioned, if Kubernetes handles the environmental variables, you do not have to update the code or restore containers if you want to adjust the variable value.

Since pods store the value of environmental variables at initialization, this is a two-step process.

Update the values first:

Kubectl build configmap language---from-literal= LANGUAGE= Spanish\-o yaml —dry-run kubectl replace-f-kubectl create the generic code apikey —from-literal= API KEУ=098765\

Then start the pods again. This can be achieved in different ways, for example by forcing a new deployment. The quick and easy way is to remove the pods manually and spin new ones automatically.

kubectl delete pod -l name=envtest

Chapter 10: Updaтing Kuвernetes Applicaтions Declaraтively

You now know how to bundle your device components into containers, group them into pods, store them temporarily or permanently, pass on secret and non-secret configuration data to them and allow pods for finding and talking with one another. You know how to run a complete system composed of smaller components–if you wish, micro-services independently. Is there anything else? Is there anything else?

You'll probably want to update your app. This chapter discusses how apps running in a Kubernetes cluster can be modified and how Kubernetes can help you move into an exact null downtime process. Though replication controllers or replica sets are the only way to do this, Kubernetes also offers a deployment tool which is situated above ReplicaSets and enables declaratory framework updates. If you don't know what that means, keep reading–it isn't as complicated as it sounds.

Updating Applications Running In Pods

Let's begin with a simple example. Consider a variety of pod cases supplying other pods and external customers with a service. After you have read this chapter, you probably know that a

ReplicationController or ReplicaSet assists these pods. There is a service that allows users (apps running on other pods or external customers) to access the pods. This is how Kubernetes looks at a simple program.

Initially, the pods run your application's first iteration–presume your picture is tagged as v1. You then create a newer version of the application and move it as a new v2 image into a picture repository. First, you would like to use this new version for all the pods. Because you can not change the image of an existing pod after the pod has been created, you need to remove and replace the old pods with new ones running the new image.

You have two ways of updating all those pods. You can do one of the following:

Then delete all existing pods and then start the new ones.

Start new ones and uninstall the old ones once they are finished. You can do this by adding all-new pods and then removing the old ones at once, or by adding new ones and slowly removing them.

Both approaches have their advantages and disadvantages. The first choice will result in a short time if your application is not available. The second option includes that your app manages two versions of the app simultaneously. If your program stores data in a data store, the new version should not change the data or the data so that the older version splits.

How do you handle these two Kubernetes update methods? Let's first explore how this is done manually, and when you know what's going on, you'll learn how to have Kubernetes update automatically.

Deleting old pods and replacing them with new ones

You also know how to get a ReplicationController to replace all its pods with new version pods. You probably remember that the ReplicationController's pod design can be modified at any time. The Replication Controller uses the modified pod design to create new instances.

If you have a ReplicationController that manages a collection of v1 pods, you can easily replace the pod template by modifying the image v2 version and then removing the old pod instances. The ReplicationController will find that its label choice does not fit, and it will spin new cases.

This is the simplest way to update a set of pods if you can embrace the brief downtime between the deletion of old and starting new pods.

This is the best way to update a collection of pods if you can embrace the brief downtime between removal and start of new pods.

Spinning up new pods and then deleting the old ones

You may turn the process around and first spin all the new pods and only then remove the old ones if you do not want to see any downtime, and your device supports multiple versions at once. More hardware is required, as you will have double the number of pods running simultaneously for a short time.

Compared to the previous approach, this is a little more complicated, but you should be able to do it by integrating what you have already heard about ReplicationControllers and Services.

Downloading from the old version to the new one at once. Generally, Pods are limited to service. You can only have the initial version of the pods at the service front when you bring up the pods running the new version. After all new pods are completed, you can switch the selector on the service label and turn the service to the new pods. This is regarded as a blue-green operation. Once you're sure that the latest version works correctly, you can delete the old pods by removing the old ReplicationController.

Take a daily test. Instead of pulling up all the new pods and removing the old pods at once, you can also update them step by step, replacing the pods. This is achieved by slowly downgrading the previous ReplicationController and upgrading it. You would want to include the old and the new pods in the Service list so that requests are guided towards both sets of pods.

The manual update is difficult and error-prone. You can execute a dozen or more commands in the appropriate order to perform the update operation, depending on the number of replicas. Fortunately, Kubernetes enables you to change the roll by a single command.

Performing An Automatic Rolling Update With A Replicationcontroller

Instead of rolling updates using ReplicationControllers, you can perform kubectl manually. Kubectl makes it much easier to upgrade the code, but as you will see later, this is an outdated method of upgrading applications. But, we'll first go through this method, because it was the first automated rolling update traditionally. It can also help us to speak about the process without adding too many new concepts.

Running the initial version of the app

You need a device deployed before you can upgrade an app. You will use a slightly modified version of the NodeJS Kubiak framework as your initial version generated in chapter 2. If you don't remember what it does, it is a simple web application that returns the hostname of the pod in the HTTP response.

Build the v1 code. You must change the software so that it returns its version number, which lets you differentiate between the various versions to be installed. Under luksa / kubia: v1, I already created and pushed the device image to Docker Hub.

Run the app and view it with a single YAML file via a server. You must build a ReplicationController and LoadBalancer to access the database externally to run your app. This time you can create a single YAML for both of them and post them to the Kubernetes API using a kubectl-create command instead of creating these two tools separately. A YAML manifest can contain many items with a line of three dashes.

The YAML describes a kubia-v1 ReplicationController and a device kubia. Go forward and post the Kubernetes YAML. You should all run three v1 pods and the load balancer after a while so that you can look up the external Address of the Server and start to hit the server with a curl.

Performing a rolling update with kubectl

Next version 2 of the app will be developed. All you will do is to change the answer by saying, "This is v2": the picture luksa / kubia: v2 in the Docker Hub contains this new version so that you do not have to create it yourself.

This latest version is available in the image luksa/kubia:v2 on Docker Hub, so you don't need to build it all yourself.

Changes to transfer the same picture attribute changes. It is not a good idea to edit an app and

move amendments to the same image tag, but we all seem to do so during development. If you change the latest tag, that is not an issue, but tagging a different tag image(such as tag v1) is a problem when the image is pulled up from a worker node, the node must store the image and not pull it back when it runs a new pod using the same image (at least this is the default image pulling policy). This means you won't make any changes to the picture if you add them to the same tag. The Kubelet will run the old version of the image if a new pod is planned for the same node.
On the other hand, nodes which did not run the old version would pull and run the new picture, so that two different versions of the pot are running. To ensure that this is not done, you must set the image pull policy property of the container to Always. You must realize that the default image pull policy is based on your image tag. If a container refers to the latest tag (or not defining it explicitly), image pull policy defaults to Always. Still, if the container refers to any other tag, IfNotPresent will be the policy default. When using any tag other than the latest one, the image pull policy must be appropriately set if you make changes to an image without modifying the tag. And better still, move a picture change under a new tag. Keep the curl loop going and open another terminal where the update rolling begins. You must run the kubectl roll-up command to

perform the update. All you need to do is tell it which ReplicationController you substitute, give the name of the new ReplicationController and decide which new image you want to replace.
You want to call the new ReplicationController kubia-v1 and use the luksa / kubia: v2 container image, as you are replacing ReplicationController kubia-v1 by one running Version 2 of your kubia app.
When you run the instruction, kubia-v2 is generated as a new ReplicationController.
The new ReplicationController's pod template references the luksa / kubia: v2 image, and its initial desired replica count is set to 0, as you can see in the following listing.
Understanding the kubectl measures before the rolling update begins. By copying the kubia-v1 controller and modifying the image in its mod prototype, Kubectl developed this ReplicationController. If you look at the label selection of the controller closely, you'll find it's modified too. It contains not only a simple app= kubia label but also a supplementary deployment label, which can be managed by this ReplicationController. Probably already know this, but this is necessary to keep both the new and the old ReplicationControllers running on the same pod set. But even if the pods created by the new controller also have an additional label for deployment, do they not indicate that they are selected by the first selector

ReplicationController, as it is set to app= kubia? Yeah, that's precisely what's going to happen, but a catch is there. The roll-up process has also updated the first ReplicationController selector.

All right, but doesn't it mean that the first controller now has zero pods that suit its selector, because the three previously created pods only contain a mark app= kubia? Yes, because also, just before modifying the ReplicationController selector kubectl changed the labels of live pods.

If this becomes too difficult to display the pods, their names, and both ReplicationControllers together with their pod selectors.

Before even attempting to scale something up or down, Kubectl had to do all this. Now imagine making the change manually. It's easy to see you wrong here, and maybe the ReplicationController can destroy all your pods — pods that support your production customers actively!

Replace old pods by scaling all ReplicationControllers with new ones. Once this has been set up, kubectl starts replacing pods by first upgrading the new controller to 1. Therefore the controller produces the first v2 stack. Then kubectl scales the old ReplicationController down by 1.

Because the Service aims at all pods with the app= kubia mark, Few loop iterations will start to see your curl requests redirected to the new v2 pod.

When kubectl continues with the rolling update, you will see a growing proportion of v2 pod requests, as the update process deletes more v1 pods and replaces them with new ones. Finally, the original ReplicationController is reduced to zero, which eliminates the last v1 pod, meaning that the Server is now only provided by v2 pods. At that point, kubectl will uninstall the original ReplicationController and complete the update process.

Now you only have the kubia-v2 ReplicationController and three v2 pods left. You have reached your service and received a response every time throughout the update process. You did a rolling update with zero downtime.

Knowing why the rolling-update of kubectl is obsolete now. I listed an even better way to update at the beginning of this section than with kubectl roll-up. What's so wrong with this method that it was better to introduce one? Okay, I don't like Kubernetes altering objects I built for one, for example. All right, it's perfectly fine if I'm going to add a node to my pods after I've created them. Still, Kubernetes changing my pod's labels and the ReplicationController label selection is something I'm not waiting for and could make me go around the office shouting to my colleagues, "Who's messing with my controllers!?"But even more importantly, if you have paid close attention to the words I have used, you probably have noticed

all this time that I specifically said that all these steps of the update were carried out by the kubectl application.
Which is the RESTful URL of your replication controller's kubia-v1 database? These are requests that your ReplicationController scales down, which indicates that the client of kubectl is the scaler instead of the master of Kubernetes. But why is it so bad that the upgrade process is done by the client rather than on the server? Okay, in your case, the update was updated smoothly, but what if you lost connectivity during the update? The update is interrupted in the center. Pods and ReplicationControllers would be intermediate. The reason why this update is not as successful as it can be is that it is imperative. Throughout this book, I have stressed how Kubernetes tells him the wished state of the system and how Kubernetes himself achieves this state by seeking out the best way. And canes are, and canes are scaled up and down. You never tell Kubernetes to add an extra pod or delete an extra pod — you change the number of replicas you want, and you want to. Similarly, in your pod descriptions, you want to modify the desired image Tag and have Kubernetes replace the pods with new ones running the new image. This is precisely why a new resource called deployment has been added, which is now the best way to deploy applications in Kubernetes.

Using Deployments For Updating Apps Declaratively

An implementation is a higher-level tool designed for deploying and upgrading applications in a declarative manner, rather than through replication controllers or replica sets, both of which are considered lower-level concepts. ReplicaSets are a new generation of ReplicationControllers, as you may recall and should be used instead. Replica sets also duplicate and control packs. When using a deployment, the actual pods are generated by the ReplicaSets of the implementation and not directly deployed.

Maybe you wonder why you would like to complicate things by placing another object on top of a ReplicationController or ReplicaSet when it is enough to keep a collection of pod instances going. As the rolling update shows, you must install an additional ReplicationController when upgrading the device and combine the two controllers to dance around the framework without stepping on the toes. You need to plan this dance. This is achieved by a deployment resource (not by the deployment resource itself, but by the process of controlling in Kubernetes). Using a deployment in place of lower-level constructs makes it much easier to update the device, as a single deployment resource specifies the desired state, and Kubernetes takes the rest of care.

Creating a Deployment

Deployment design is not so different from the creation of the ReplicationController. A deployment also consists of a label generator, a specified number of replicas, and a pod prototype. It also includes an area defining a deployment strategy that specifies how an upgrade should be performed when the deployment resource is updated.

Establishing a form of deployment. See how to use the kubia-v1 ReplicationController example in this chapter earlier and change it to represent the deployment instead of a ReplicationController. As you will see, only three trivial changes are required.

Since you had previously controlled a particular variant of the pods, you renamed it kubia-v1. A release is above that version stuff, on the other hand. At one time, several pod versions running under its wing may be deployed, so its name should not apply to the app version.

Providing the tool for deployment. Make sure you uninstall any ReplicationControllers and pods that are still running until you build this deployment, but keep the kubia service now. You can use the —all option to disable all such Replication Controllers.

You're now set to create your Deployment.

Displaying the rollout deployment status. You can use the regular kubectl deployed, and the kubectl commands explain how to implement, but allow me to direct you to an additional command specifically made to check the status of the deployment.

Understand how Deploys build ReplicaSets that construct the pods. Take note of these pods ' names. Before, if you were using a ReplicationController to build pods, their names had the controller's name plus a randomly generated string (e.g., kubia-v1-m33mv). In the center of the deployment, the three pods provide an additional numerical value. What exactly is that? The number is equivalent to the hashed value in the implementation of the pod prototype and the ReplicaSet that manages these pods. As we said before, deployment does not explicitly control pods. Instead, it generates and leaves the ReplicaSets to handle, so let's look at the ReplicaSet generated by your implementation: the name replicaSet also contains its pod template hash value. As you'll see later, several ReplicaSets are generated for each version of the pod prototype by a deployment. Using the hash value of the pod template like this, the implementation will always use the same replicaSet (possibly available) for a particular version of the pod template.

Connect the pods via the software. With the three replicas that have now been created by this

ReplicaSet, you can use the service that you created earlier to access them because you made new pods ' labels to fit the selector label of the service. Until then, you've still not seen enough reasons why you should use Deployments over ReplicationControllers. Fortunately, it was also no harder to create a deployment than to build a ReplicationController. Now, with this deployment, you can start doing things, which will explain why implementations are superior. In the next few moments, this becomes apparent when you see how updating your device via a deployment tool is comparable to updating it with a ReplicationController.

Updating a Deployment

In the past, you had to explicitly tell Kubernetes to update your device using a ReplicationController by using a kubectl rolling update. You even had to insert the name to replace the old ReplicationController. At the end of the process, Kubernetes substituted all original pods with new ones and removed the original ReplicationController. During the process, you had to stick around, keep your terminal open, and wait for kubectl to update.

Compare this now with how you will upgrade the deployment. The only thing you need to do is to modify the deployment resource's pod template, and Kubernetes will take all necessary steps to make the actual system status as specified in the document. Just like scaling up or down a ReplicationController, all you need to do is refer to a new image tag in the Deployment Pod Set and let it adapt to Kubernetes to suit your device to a new desired state.

Chapter 11: Deploying Replicated Stateful Applications

The MySQL example is a ConfigMap, two Services, and a StatefulSet.

ConfigMap Generates the YAML settings file for ConfigMap.

This ConfigMap includes my.cnf overrides, which allows you to control configuration independently on the MySQL master and slaves. In this situation, you want the master to be able to slave replication logs and slaves to reject all writings that do not come from replication.

There is nothing unique about the ConfigMap itself, which causes various portions to apply to multiple Pods. -Pod determines which part to consider, based on the information given by the controller StatefulSet.

Services

Creates the Services from the following YAML file: You should see all 3 Pods running after a while:

NAME	READY	STATUS	RESTARTS	AGE
Mysql-0	2/2	Running	0	2m
Mysql-1	2/2	Running	0	1m
mysql-2	2/2	Running	0	1m

To cancel the watch, press Ctrl+C. If you see no improvement, make sure you have a PersistentVolume dynamic supplier that is disabled as specified in the conditions.

This manifest uses a variety of techniques to handle stately pods in a StatefulSet. The following section discusses some of these strategies to illustrate how StatefulSet produces poods.

Understanding Stateful Pod Initialization

The StatefulSet controller begins Pods one by one, according to their standard index. It is waiting until every Pod report is ready before the next one begins.

Furthermore, the controller assigns each Pod a single, stable type name <statefulset-name>-<ordinal-index > resulting in Pods called mysql-0, mysql-1 and mysql-2.

The Pod template in the above StatefulSet manifest utilizes these properties to continue MySQL replication in an orderly manner.

Generating configuration

Before you start any of the Pod spec containers, the Pod will first run any original containers in the specified order.

Init-MySQL, the first init folder, creates unique MySQL configuration files based on the ordinal index.

The script calculates its ordinal index by extracting it from the end of the Pod name that the hostname command returns. Then it stores the ordinal in a file called server-id.cnf on the MySQL conf.d directory (with a numeric offset to avoid reserved values). This translates the particular, secure identity of the StatefulSet controller into the MySQL server ID domain that needs the same property.

The script in the container init-MySQL will also refer to master.cnf or slave.cnf of the ConfigMap if the text is copied to conf.d. Because the topology example consists of a single MySQL master and all the slaves, the script only assigns ordinal0 as the master and everybody else as slaves. Combined with the deployment order guarantee of the StatefulSet server, this guarantees that the MySQL master is ready before the slave creation process can start replicating.

Cloning existing data

When a new Pod is added to the set as a slave, it must generally assume that the

MySQL master may already have data on it. It must also presume that replication logs can not go back to the start of time. Such conservative assumptions are the key to allow a running StatefulSet to scale up and down over time instead of set to its original size.

The second Init container, known as clone-MySQL, conducts a slave Pod clone operation the first time it begins in an empty PersistentVolume. It ensures that it copies all existing data from another running Pod so that their local condition is sufficiently consistent with duplicating the master.

MySQL alone does not provide a framework for this reason, so the example uses Percona XtraBackup, a standard open-source tool. During the replication, the MySQL server source could be degraded. To minimize its effect on the MySQL master, the script instructs any Pod to clone from the Pod with a lower ordinal number. It works since Pod N is always ready before beginning Pod N+1 with the StatefulSet controller.

Starting replication

After the Init Containers have been completed successfully, the containers run regularly. The MySQL Pods are composed of a MySQL container running the new MySQL server and an extra backup container serving as a sidecar.

The extra backup sidecar looks at the cloned data files and decides whether MySQL slave replication needs to be initialized. If this is the case, it waits for mysqld and executes the CHANGE MASTER TO and START SLAVE commands with XtraBackup clone replication parameters.

When a slave replicates, it restores its MySQL master and immediately reconnects if the server restarts or the connection dies. Since slaves search for the master on their secure DNS name (MySQL-0.mysql), they will find the master automated, even if the master gets a new Pod Address.

Finally, the extra backup container listens to connections from other Pods requesting a data clone after replication has begun. This server remains up indefinitely if the StatefulSet is up or if the next Pod loses the PersistentVolumeClaim, and the clone has to be re-done.

Sending client traffic

You can send test queries to the MySQL master by running a temporary container with MySQL:5.7 and using the binary client MySQL.

Clubbuj-client mysqul —image= mysql:5.7 —i-rm—restart= Never—\Mysql-h mysql-0.mysql < EOF DATABASE test; CREATE TABLE test.messages (message VARCHAR(250));

Make use of the hostname mysql-read to send test queries to any server that reports being Ready:

kubectl runs mysql-client —image= mysql:5.7—t —rm —restart= NEVER—\mysql-h mysql-read

You should get output like this:

Waiting for a pod default / MySQL-client to run, status is pending.

```
+---------+
| Message |
+---------+
| Hello   |
+---------+
```

Pod "mysql-client" deleted

To demonstrate that the MySQL-read Service distributes connections through servers, you can run SELECT @@server I.D in a loop, see @@server I.D modification because each link seeks to select another endpoint.

If you want to interrupt the loop, you can press Ctrl+C, but to keep it going, it is useful to see the results of the following steps.

Simulating Pod And Node Downtime

If you want to interrupt the loop, you can press Ctrl+C, but to keep it going, it is useful to see the results of the following steps.

Split the Preparation Probe

The MySql database preparation probe runs the MySQL command-h 127.0.0.1 -e' SELECT 1' to make sure the server is up and able to run queries.

One way to break the readiness probe is: kubectl exec MySQL-2-c MySQL— mv /usr / bin / MySQL /usr / bin / MySQL off It hits the real Pod MySQL-2 container file system and renames the MySQL command so that the readiness probe can't find it. The Pod will declare one of its containers not ready after a matter of seconds, which can be tested by running:

Kubectl gets pod MySQL-2 Lookup to 1/2 in the READY column:

READY STATUS RESTARTS AGE MySQL-2 1/2 Running 0 3 m

You should still see your @@server I d Pick loop, even if it's never reporting 102 more. Remember, the server-id specified by the unit-MySQL script is 100+$ordinal, and thus the server ID 102 is Pod MySQL-2.

Now repair the Pod and it should reappear in the loop output after a few seconds:

kubectl exec mysql-2 -c mysql -- mv /usr/bin/mysql.off /usr/bin/mysql

Delete Pods

The StatefulSet recreates poods if it is removed as a ReplicaSet does for stateless poods.

The StatefulSet controller finds no longer exists a MySQL-2 Pod and creates a new one with the same name and connection to the same persistent volume claim. You should see Server ID 102 vanish for a while from the loop output and return for yourself.

Drain a Node

If you have several nodes in your Kubernetes cluster, you can simulate downtime of nodes (e.g., when nodes are updated) by emitting a drain.

First decide on which one of the MySQL Pods Node is: kubectl get pod MySQL-2-o big In the last tab, the node name will show up:

NAME READY STATUS RESTARTS AGE IP NODE

Mysql-2 2/2 Running 0 15 m 10.244.5.27 Kubernetes-node-9l2 t Run an order, which cords to prevent any new Pods from planning and then eliminates any of the current Pods.

Replace the Node name you find in the last stage with < node-name>.

This could affect other node applications, so only in a test cluster is best done.

Kubectl drain < node-name >—force —delete-local-data —ignore-daemon sets Now you can see the Pod reschedules on another Node: kubectl can get the MySQL-2-wide –watch edition.

And again, you should see that Server ID 102 disappears for a while from the output of SELECT @@server I d and then returns.

The node is now incorporated to restore it to a reasonable condition: kubectl un cordon < node-name >

Scaling The Number Of Slaves

You can scale your read query ability by adding slaves with MySQL replication. You can do this using a single command: kubectl scale stateful set MySQL— replicas=5 Look at the new Pods by running: kubectl get pods-l app= MySQL-watch Once they're up you should see the SELECT @@server I.D loop output server IDs 103-104 start.

You can also guarantee that the data you had placed on these new servers before they existed:

Scaling back down remains seamless:

kubectl scale stateful set MySQL— replicas=3
Remember, however, that scaling down does not automatically remove these PVC's while scaling up produces the current PersistentVolumeClaims. It allows you to keep the configured PVCs around for faster scale backup or extract data before removing them. This can be seen by using: kubectl gets PVC-l app= MySQL, which shows all 5 PVCs still exist, even though the StatefulSet has been reduced to 3.

You should uninstall the extra PVCs if you do not want to reuse them: kubectl delete data-MySQL-3 kubectl delete PVC data-MySQL-4.

Cleaning up

Cancel the SELECT @@server I.D loop by pressing the Ctrl + C button or by running the following from a different terminal:

Erase the StatefulSet. This also helps to end the Pods.

Remove statefulset MySQL kubectl

Verify the Pods are gone. It might take some time to finish.

Kubectl gets pods-l application= MySQL.

You'll know the Pods have terminated when the above returns:

Erase the Services and PersistentVolumeClaims, ConfigMap.

kubectl delete configmap, service, PVC –l app= MySQL–presume you also have to manually remove PersistentVolumes, as well as to unlock the underlying tools. If you use a dynamic provisioner, the PersistentVolumes will be deleted automatically when you see the PersistentVolumeClaims have been removed. Some dynamic suppliers (for example, EBS and PD) often release the underlying resources when the PersistentVolumes has been removed.

Chapter 12: Understanding Kubernetes Internals

When you use a traditional VM, you have access to ssh in a fixed instance with a public IP assigned and configured to which the DNS that resolve. After the DNS has been set to solve your hostname, you can install certbot on it and generate the certificates in that case.

Things get a bit tricky with Kubernetes. You will still have some instances in your cluster, but they are not available directly from outside the cluster. Moreover, you can not prevent your Nginx or other entrance nodes from operating. So the easiest way to set up the system is by using Kubernetes and dockers. This also gives us some advantages:

As part of the Kubernetes manifest files and Dockerfiles, our solution will function for any number of pods and services. The cert generation process is recorded. Ultimately, we will not get stuck because of problems due to scalability, such as adding additional pods or even adding more nodes to our cluster. Things are going to work seamlessly until a new cluster is formed.

Solution, like dockers and Kubernetes, is an independent network. This runs on any GCP, AWS, or even Azure cloud service (hopefully). Now we have the static IP, and we can switch to a fun part of the Kubernetes.

The Loadbalancer Service

The first thing that we set up is the load balance software, and we will then use this service to fix our certbot customer's pods and then our app pods.

Most of it is self explanatory, few fields of interest are:

spec.type: This spins a Google cloud into GCP and AWS Elastic into AWS spec. — It assigns previously created static IP. Now all traffic to our IP address is split into this.

Ports.port–We have opened two TCP ports, port 80 and port 443, respectively, to facilitate HTTP and HTTPS traffic.

Spec.selector–These are labels that allow us to determine which pods should refer to. Later on, we will use the same label collection in our Work and Pod templates

Let's deploy this service to our cluster.

If we see the status of our service now, we should see this.

Next we have to think about where to run our certbot container.

Job Controllers

The work inspectors at Kubernetes help to prepare the finishing touches. In other words, these are tasks that will not have to be carried out again in the future if they are done without mistake. That's precisely what we want when we generate SSL certificates. So soon as the certbot process is completed and certificates are issued, this container no longer needs to be run. We don't want Kubernetes to restart this node, too. Nevertheless, when a failure/error occurs, we can ask Kubernetes to reprogram the pod automatically.

You can, therefore, enter a Job specimen file using certbot to create the SSL cert. Certbot provides a container that can only be reused in our case for docking.

Few important fields here are:

Spec.template.metadata.labels-This refers to the spec.selector of our LoadBalancer service. This puts our load balancer under our load. Everything on port 80 and port 443 will now be drunk to our bowl.

The image of a certbot / certbot docker is spec.template.spec.containers[0].image.
Kubernetes pulls the certbot / certbot docker on the server for us when this pod is scheduled.
spec.template.spec.containers[0].command-The pod command.
Spec.template.spec.containers[0].args-The above command arguments. We use the standalone certbot mode to generate certain items here as it makes things simple. In certbot documentation spec.template.spec.containers[0].ports you can learn more about this order-Port 80 and 443 are available for the containers.

Where to save the SSL certificate generated?
We currently have two options to save the certificates: Save it in an activated number. (Not recommended)
If a PersistentVolume would be needed and a PersistentVolumeClaim
The certificate could only be some KB in size, but GKE allots a minimum volume of 1Gi. This is also highly inefficient.

Use kubernetes Secrets. (Recommended)

This would also allow us to use the cluster configuration of the Kubernetes client, which is typically the recommended way to use it. Would we need to configure ClusterRole and ClusterRoleBinding?

Can be configured to permit access by RBAC (RoleBasedAccessControl) to specific people

Why in-cluster access?

To understand this, we have to go into our current architecture a little deeper.

The certificates created by our Job Controller Pod are already inside the cluster, as we can see. We want to store these certified certificates in secrets.

If secrets are collected/created/modified in normal flow, it typically is done by the kubectl client.

The generation of certificates was successful. We really can't write to Secrets, though. It is shown by the last line in the above production.

Secrets are prohibited: User "system: service account: default: default" can not build secrets in a "normal" namespace.

Why is that? Because

RBAC or Role-Based Access Control in Kubernetes consists of 2 parts: Role / ClusterRole RoleBinding / ClusterRoleBinding The ClusterRole and the ClusterRoleBinding method are used to provide our Pod with large cluster access. The Function and RoleBinding method, which can be used by the docs– https:/kubernetes.io/docs/reference/access-authn-authz/rbac/Fields of interest, herein are.subjects can provide more finely oriented, function-based access. It's an array, and in that, we've identified two forms.

Type: User: This refers to the current user who uses kubectl to execute these orders. This is required to give the current user appropriate permissions in which to grant the.rules. Resources and.rules.verbs access relevant to the ClusterRole definitions we have described in RBAC-cr.yml.

Species: ServiceAccount: This applies to the use of the account within the cluster while our pot generates the secrets with the proxy.

Chapter 13: Securing Tнe Kuвernetes Api Server

The growing component must be carefully protected so that the integrity of the cluster is maintained overall.

Cluster Installers

We will start with a brief comment on the many different tools to install the components of the cluster.

Some of the default parameters of the configuration of the components of the Kubernetes cluster are unsafe and must be set correctly to ensure that the cluster is stable. If you opt for a controlled Kubernetes (for example, Giant Swarm) cluster where you control the entire cluster, the many different cluster deployment tools available, each with a subtly different configuration, exacerbates the problem. While many installers come with reasonable defaults, we should never think of our backs as regards safety and make it our task to ensure that any installer system we choose to use is designed to protect the cluster from suiting the requirements.

Let's look at some of the important safety aspects of the control aircraft.

API Server

The API server is the center of all communication within the cluster, and most security configurations are implemented on the API server. The API server is the only part of the control plane of the cluster, which can interact directly with the state storage of the cluster. Users running the cluster, other control plane components, and cluster workloads often communicate with the cluster using the HTTP-based REST API of the server. Due to its vital position in control of the cluster, it is crucial to carefully monitor access to the API server in terms of security. When someone or something has unauthorized access to the API, they may accumulate all sorts of sensitive information and gain control of the cluster itself. User access to the Kubernetes API should, therefore, be encrypted, authenticated, and allowed.

Securing Communication with TLS

To avoid man-in-the-middle attacks, TLS should encrypt the communication between all clients and the API servers. To do this, the API server needs a private key and X.509 certificate to be configured.

Every client who has to authenticate to an API server during a TLS handshake must have the X.509 Root Certificate Authority (CA) certificate provided by an API server, which contributes to a general question of certificate bodies for that cluster. As we'll soon see, clients can authenticate to the API server in numerous ways, one of which is via X.509 certificates. When this approach, which is possibly true in most cases (at least for the cluster components), is used, then every cluster component should be granted its certificate, and the establishment of a cluster-wide PKI capability is very important.

There are several ways to achieve a PKI capability for a cluster and no better way than another. This can be configured manually, or by some other means, with the help of your chosen installer. Indeed, the cluster can be set up to have its own integrated CA, which can issue certificates in response to signing requests sent via the API server. We use an operator called cert-operator here at Giant Swarm in tandem with Hashicorp's Vault.

While it's a matter of secure communication with the API server, make sure you disable the unsecured port (before Kubernetes 1.13) serving the API via a simple (—insecure-port=0) HTTP!

Authentication, Authorization, and Admission Control

Now let us concentrate on testing which customers can conduct which operations which cluster resources. We're not going to go into much depth here, as this is primarily a topic for the next post. The important thing is to ensure that the control plane components are designed to provide the underlying access controls.

When an API requires lands on an API server, it performs a series of checks to decide whether or not the request is to be fulfilled and whether the resource object is validated or mutated in compliance with the specified policy. The execution chain is shown in the diagram above.

Kubernetes supports many different authentication mechanisms, most of them implemented outside the cluster. These include X.509 certificates, simple auth, bearer tokens, OpenID Connect (OIDC). The different systems are allowed with the corresponding configuration options on the API server, so make sure you supply them for your authentication scheme(s). X.509 Client

Certificate Authentication requires a file path that includes, for instance, one or more CAs (—client-ca-file) certificates. One important point to remember is that any API requests not authenticated by any authentication system are regarded as anonymous requests by default. Although access to unknown applications may be restricted by permission, if not necessary, they should be disabled (—anonymous-auth= false).

The API server considers the demand against authorization policy once a request is authenticated. Again, authorization modes are a(—authorization mode) configuration option, which should at least be changed to the AlwaysAllow default value. Ideally, RBAC and Node should be included in the authorization modes list, for example, the RBAC API for fine-grained access control, and kubelet API requests should be approved (see below).

Once an API request is authenticated and approved, the resource object can be validated or mutated with the admission controller before persisting in the cluster's state database. For use, a minimum set of admission controllers should not be removed from the list unless there is a very good reason for doing so. Specific admission controllers relevant to the protection that are worth considering are:

DenyEscalatingExec — this admission controller will prevent users from executing commands on a pod's privileged containers if your pods need to be allowed to run with enhanced privileges (for example, using IPC / PID namespaces from the host).

PodSecurityPolicy — provides the means to enforce different safety policies for all produced pods. In our next article in this series, we shall discuss that further, but it is important to ensure that this admission controller is allowed at this time. Otherwise, the security policy cannot be enforced.

NodeRestriction— an admittance controller that controls the access of a cluster has to cluster resources that are listed further below.

ImagePolicyWebhook — allows an external "Image Validator" such as the Image Enforcer to search for vulnerabilities in images specified for a pods ' containers. Centered on the Open Policy Agent (OPA), Image Enforcer works in tandem with the Clair open source vulnerability scanner.

A relatively new feature in Kubernetes, dynamic intake control, aims to provide much more flexibility over the static plugin intake control mechanism. It is introduced with webhooks and controller-based initializers and promises much for cluster security as soon as community solutions mature enough.

Kubelet

The kubelet is an agent running at each node on the cluster and responsible for all pod-related activities on the node it operates, including start / stop and restart pod containers, reporting on the health of pod containers. After the API server, the kubelet is the next cluster portion for security consideration.

Accessing the Kubelet REST API

A small REST API is given in the kubelet on ports 10250 and 10255. Port 10250 is a read/write port, while port 10255 is a read-only port with an API endpoint subset.

Providing unlimited access to port 10250 is dangerous because arbitrary commands can be executed within container pods, and arbitrary pods can be started. Likewise, both ports provide read-access to the potentially sensible pod and container information that may make workloads susceptible to compromises. The read-only port should be de-set by setting the configuration of the kubelet—read-only-port=0 to protect against possible compromise. Nonetheless, for the collection of metrics and other critical functions, Port 10250 must be open. Access to this port should be carefully controlled, so let's talk about key configurations of protection.

Client Authentication

The kubelet API is available for unauthenticated client requests unless expressly configured. Consequently, it is important to set one of the authentication methods available; X.509 client certificates or applications with Authorization headers containing bearer tokens.

The contents of a CA package must be available to the cubelet in the case of customer certificates X.509 so that certificates submitted by customers can be authenticated during the TLS handshake. This is supported as part of the kubelet (—client-ca-file) setup.

In an ideal world, the Kubernetes API server is the only client that needs access to a Kubernetes API. For various functions like logging and measurements, executing a command in a container (think kubectl exec), forwarding a port in a container, etc. You need to access the kubelet API endpoints. The API server must be configured using TLS Client (—-kubelet-client-certificate and —kubelet-client-key) to authenticate the kubelet.

Anonymous Authentication

You can be forgiven for thinking "work done" if you have taken care to set up the API server's access to the kubelet's API. But that is not the case, as requests that hit the kubelet's API, which does not seek to authenticate the kubelet, are considered anonymous. In essence, the kubelet transfers anonymous authorization requests by default instead of refusing it as unauthenticated.

If anonymous kubelet API applications are required in your environment, the authorization gate offers some flexibility to decide what the API can and can not do with. However, it's much easier to disclaim anonymous API requests by making the—anonymous-authentic configuration of the kubelet fake. The API returns a 401 unauthorized response to unauthorized clients with this configuration.

Authorization

With authorization requests for the kubelet API, a default Kubernetes setting can again be abused. Kubelet API authorization operates in two modes; Always Allow (default) or Webhook. The Always Allow mode does exactly what you would expect-it allows the authentication gate to succeed all requests that have passed. It requires anonymous applications.

The best approach is to download the authorization decision to the Kubernetes API server using the kubelet —authorization-mode config option, with Webhook meaning, instead of leaving it wide open. With this configuration, the kubelet calls the SubjectAccessReview API to decide whether or not a subject can make a request. This configuration is part of the API server.

Restricting the Power of the Kubelet

In earlier Kubernetes versions (previous to 1.7), the kubelet had read-write access to all node and Pod API objects, even if the Node and Pod objects had control over another node. They also accessed all objects in pod specs: Hidden, ConfigMap, PersistentVolume, and PersistentVolumeClaim objects. In other words, a kubelet had access to and control of many resources for which it was not responsible. This is effective, and the damage will quickly escalate beyond the node in question in the event of a compromise in the cluster node.

Node Authorizer

Therefore, an explicitly designed kubelet node authorization mode to control its access to the Kubernetes API has been added. The Node authorizer restricts the kubeles to read operations for things about kubelets (e.g., pods, nodes, services) and applies additional read-only limits to Secrets, Configmap, PersistentVolume, and persistent volume claim artifacts.

NodeRestriction Admission Controller

Limiting a kubelet to read-only access for the related objects is a big step towards avoiding a broken cluster or workload. Nevertheless, the cubelet needs writing access to its Node and Pod objects as a way of its normal function. To make this possible, after a node authorization request has passed the kubelet API test, the kubelet is then subject to the NodeRestriction admission controller restricting the node and pod objects that can be modified by kubelet, itself. To do this, the kubelet user should be a system: node:<nodeName >, which must belong to the group system: nodes. It is the kubelet user NodeName part that is used by the NodeRestriction input controller to permit or disallow kubelet API requests that modify node and pude artifacts. Therefore, each cubelet should have a unique X.509 certificate for authentication to the API server with the common name and organization of the topic separated by the user name.

Once again, these essential configurations do not happen automatically, and the API server must be started as one of the —authorization-mode configuration plug-in list with the node as a commas-defined list, while NodeRestriction needs to be on the —enable-admission-plugin list of entry controllers listed.

Best Practice

We have only covered a subset of security considerations for the cluster layer (although necessary), and if you think all this sounds exceptionally overwhelming, then don't be afraid because assistance is accessible.

Just like benchmark safety guidelines for network layer elements such as Docker have been developed for a Kubernetes cluster. The Internet Security Center (CIS) has compiled a full set of configuration settings and file system inspections, published as the CIS Cubanets Benchmark, for each node of the cluster.

You may also want to find out that the Kubernetes group has created an open-source tool to audit a Kubernetes benchmark, the Kubernetes Security Bench. It is a Golang program and supports various Kubernetes versions (1.6 onwards) and different benchmark versions.

If you want to protect your cluster correctly, then use the benchmark as a measure of compliance is a must.

Conclusion

Kubernetes ' main strength is its modularity and generality. Almost any device you want to deploy will fit into Kubernetes and, regardless of the type of modification or tuning you need to make to your system, it's usually possible. This modularity and generality are expensive, and this expense is a fair amount of complexity. Knowing how the APIs and components in Kubernetes operate is important to effectively release Kubernetes ' power to simplify, manage, and deploy your application. Also, recognizing how Kubernetes is connected to a wide range of external systems and processes such as an on-premise database and a continuous delivery system is essential for using Kubernetes effectively and in the real world. Throughout this book, we have worked to provide practical, real-life experience on specific matters you would probably meet if you are a beginner. No matter if you face a new field where you need to become an expert, or you want to revisit how others have tackled the familiar problem, hopefully, the chapters in this book have allowed you to benefit from our experience. We do hope that you gain the skills and motivation to make full use of Kubernetes.

As the enthusiasm for Kubernetes in the development community has persisted, valid criticism of Kubernetes for its huge learning curve and overhead needed to maintain the animal has been made. Very few businesses have problems with Google size to solve by Kubernetes. Nevertheless, at Leverege, we achieved tangible benefits in terms of auto-scaling, self-healing, immutability, cross-platform compatibility, and more straightforward deployment once infrastructure was set up.

Given the unique challenges of the developing IoT environment, Kubernetes has made a significant contribution to the Leverege team by the DevOps tools (deployment, tracking, management of incidents). As more and more resources in the Kubernetes ecosystem are standardized to improve security, visibility, and usability, Leverege is confident in the importance Kubernetes has for IoT-grade production deployments.

Kubernetes is an excellent instrument for orchestration of containerized applications. It automates the very complex task of scaling an application dynamically in real-time. The problem with K8s is that it's a complex system; it works when things don't work as planned. It is essential to monitor both the Kubernetes and the application environment(s) to ensure that everything works as it should and that application users are provided with fast and error-free service. The monitoring approach has to offer both the Kubernetes cluster and the applications it serves with an integrated view. It must always be able to adapt to the constantly changing world as workloads are distributed through many nodes. It must be able to ingest vast amounts of data: time series, events, and traces, and then condense them into operational data. If you currently have K8s or intend to use them to handle applications based on your production containers, you need to test Instana. The entire stack, including orchestration and containers, was designed to monitor. Kubernetes is a complex framework with minimal functionality. As previously stated, it aims to deploy, scale, and manage containers (such as Docker), which run custom applications ' components. If you intend to use it to manage your production applications, it is important to understand Kubernetes ' overall architecture.

www.ingramcontent.com/pod-product-compliance
Lightning Source LLC
Chambersburg PA
CBHW071122050326
40690CB00008B/1308

* 9 7 8 1 7 7 8 0 5 7 9 4 6 *